Who doesn't love the dark side? You know you do! To_____ DePalma — everybody loves a great villain. Pamela _____ gives you the tools to harness this wild horse and make your scripts come alive with *The Power of the Dark Side*.
    — Ellen Sandler, Former Co-Executive Producer of "Everybody Loves Raymond" and author of *The TV Writer's Workbook* (Bantam/Dell)

Well, Pamela Jaye Smith has done it again. Your hero is only as good as the antagonist she's fighting. In exploring the power of the Dark Side, Smith has provided all the tools you'll need to define the villain of your piece. The rest is up to you.
    — Bruce Logan, A.S.C., Emmy-winning Writer/Director, Cameraman
    www.bruceloganfilm.com

Every once in a while, an exceptional book comes along -- such is Pamela Jaye Smith's latest offering, *The Power of the Dark Side*. She not only defines "bad" and "evil," but deftly gives us examples from all creative corners, explaining the genesis, the characteristics, and the mythological and psychological underpinnings which can take your storytelling to a whole new stratosphere! What makes this book such a standout is Smith's winning writing style, which provides us with an entertaining "read" as well as a treasure trove of information which writers can continue to rely upon for decades!
    — Kathie Fong Yoneda, Seminar Leader, Producer, Author of *THE SCRIPT-SELLING GAME: An Hollywood Insider's Look at Getting Your Script Sold and Produced*

The Power of the Dark Side is essential reading for writers in all genres who want to authentically portray the quality and power of evil in their characters. Pamela Jaye Smith writes in a highly entertaining style that displays a profound breadth of knowledge from many disciplines.
    — Celeste Allegrea Adams, Screenwriter, Story Consultant
    www.CreatrixStudio.com

Pamela Jaye Smith has brought screenwriting to a whole new level! Her mythical approach to story and screenwriting has deepened our understanding of conflict and villains and antagonists, and even how to work with the problem of evil. Rich with concepts, examples, and possibilities, any writer would find this helpful in adding dimension and credibility and depth to their characters. This is a book to be read and reread and worked with. Fill the margins of this book with ideas and thoughts... read slowly and often! And besides, you'll love Pamela's wit and humor! I laughed out loud more than once!
    — Dr. Linda Seger, Script Consultant, Author, Screenwriting Teacher

As an actor, writer, and video game designer, I've found *The Power of the Dark Side* enormously useful. The exercises in this book have enabled me to create much more powerful characters, as both protagonists and antagonists, to say nothing of the ever-favorite anti-hero. Plus, it's a fun read!
    — Aurora Miller, Games Industry professional, JAMDAT Mobile, Electronic Arts

It's a fact that the more multifaceted, clever, and resourceful the bad guy is in your story, the more mulitfaceted, clever, and resourceful the hero has to be to defeat him... which means a better film for the audience. Pamela Jaye Smith's insights in *The Power of the Dark Side* will inspire you to create villains truly worthy of all the silvery screens.
    — Steven A. Finly, WGAw, *Wishful Thinking, Blackheart, In Her Mother's Footsteps*

I found Pamela Jaye Smith's *Power of the Dark Side* to be of tremendous assistance in the development process of our supernatural thriller feature film project, especially in the area of creating believable villainy.

— Lynn Hendee, Producer, Chartoff Productions

In *The Power of the Dark Side*, Pamela Jaye Smith has once again honed in on the salient and vital points so often overlooked by both veteran and novice writers when constructing a masterpiece to entice and enthrall producers and audiences alike. Whether you're creating a character we love to hate, designing one of those bad boys (or girls) we can't help but be drawn to, or trying to convey the age-old "the devil made me do it," this book is a must-have and a must-read for everyone in the writing business.

— Lynn Santer, Author, Screenwriter, and Conservationist
   www.lynnsanter.com, www.themagicalscarecrows.com

This book is an invaluable resource for anyone involved in the creative side of the video game business. The ultimate test of a game is that it contains exciting gameplay – gripping challenges for the player to overcome. Unfortunately, the physical challenges offered in most games are unimaginative and predictable; and as for the bad guys, they are usually stereotypes we've seen a hundred times before... Pamela Jaye Smith's book is full of excellent ideas on how to create dramatic obstacles and unique, powerful, fully dimensional antagonists.

— Carolyn Handler Miller, Writer and consultant for video games and other forms
   of interactive media; author of *Digital Storytelling: A Creator's Guide to Interactive
   Entertainment* (Focal Press)

The Power of the Dark Side is a fascinating book, filled with incredible information for anyone, not only writers, interested in the Dark Side of life. Pamela Jaye Smith has the ability and knowledge to take complex material and make it accessible to readers. She not only gives writers many new tools to make characters dark and stories dramatic, but she also illustrates how the dark side affects us in our universe. Congratulations on a terrific book that illuminates the power of the Dark Side in all of us.

— Rachel Ballon, Ph.D., Writer's psychotherapist in private practice, international
   writing consultant and author of five books on writing, the latest, *The Writer's
   Portable Therapist: 25 Sessions to a Creativity Cure*

"*The Power of the Dark Side* is an incredible exploration of the different dimensions of Evil. Pamela Jaye Smith demonstrates once again that she is one of the world's experts, not only on multicultural mythology but also on the application of the ideas of archetype, symbol, and cognitive science. While she's written this book with the writer in mind, her exploration of the ideas of evil will be of great value to teachers, therapists, and anyone who deals with people, education, motivation, or persuasion. For writers, it opens up a world of ideas that will help in building more complex antagonists. To have a great hero, you need a great villain. *Dark Side* delivers far more than you'd expect from one book."

— Rob Kall, publisher of *OpEdNews.com* and founder, Storycon Summit Meeting
   on the Art, Science and Application of Story

"What Joseph Campbell did to explain myth, Pamela Jaye Smith does to help us understand human menace. She reveals the crucial role of disturbing characters in mythic structure. This is the best guide ever to creating believable villains. The reader also gains a fuller understanding of personal shadow. This illuminating work will be a much-used addition to the writer's bookshelf."

— Jonathan Young, PhD, Psychologist, Founding Curator, Joseph Campbell
   Archives

THE POWER
OF THE
DARK SIDE

CREATING GREAT VILLAINS,
DANGEROUS SITUATIONS,
& DRAMATIC CONFLICT

⮜BY⮞

PAMELA JAYE SMITH

MICHAEL WIESE PRODUCTIONS

Published by Michael Wiese Productions
3940 Laurel Canyon Blvd. – Suite 1111
Studio City, CA 91604
(818) 379-8799, (818) 986-3408 (FAX).
mw@mwp.com
www.mwp.com

Cover design by MWP
Interior design by William Morosi
Copyedited by Adria Carey
Printed by McNaughton & Gunn

Manufactured in the United States of America

Library of Congress Cataloging-in-Publication Data
Smith, Pamela Jaye, 1948-
  The power of the dark side : creating great villains, dangerous situations, & dramatic
conflict / Pamela Jaye Smith.
       p. cm.
  Includes bibliographical references and index.
  ISBN-13: 978-1-932907-43-8
  ISBN-10: 1-932907-43-2
  1. Motion picture authorship. 2. Villains in literature. 3. Evil in literature. I. Title.
  PN1996.S59 2008
  808.3'97--dc22

                          2008009401

Printed on Recycled Stock

DEDICATION

TO

BOGIE, BRUCE, MICHAEL, MONTY, REX, RICK

WARRIORS, WIZARDS, WONDERS

TABLE OF CONTENTS

ACKNOWLEDGEMENTS

For inspiring and guiding my fascination with how the Dark Side works, I owe infinite gratitude to Georgia Lambert, an amazing Wisdom Teacher and Instructor in Defense Against the Dark Arts.

Special thanks go to my content contributors. Monty Hayes McMillan helped brainstorm the book and clarify the concepts. He explained a lot of the groupthink categories, and he offered many of the movie examples. Geffrey von Gerlach, novelist and Doctor of Oriental Medicine, offered expertise in witching ways and all things magical. Michael Wilson Woods instructed me in philosophies and mechanics of the martial arts. Aurora Miller added relevant insights from the world of computer games. Major General Lon E. Maggart and Colonel Tom Dempsey (both U.S. Army, retired) schooled me in many ways of war and intelligence. In addition, long, varied, and fascinating conversations with many friends over many years contributed insights and observations on the Dark Side and its effects.

Feedback and suggestions from many generous readers were invaluable in crafting this book. Special gratitude to Jill Gurr, Monty Hayes McMillan, Steve Finly, Kathie Fong Yoneda, Linda Seger, Geffrey von Gerlach, Mario Bernheim, Aurora Miller, Judith Claire, Brian Dyer, Pam Shepard, Pierre Debs, Michele Shourt, Bruce Logan, James Atticus Bowden, and Dermot Davis.

For their vision and support, my publishers Michael Wiese and Ken Lee, along with copy editor Adria Carey, layout artist Bill Morosi, and the rest of the fine MWP team.

We must all also thank all storytellers who create the myths, fairy tales, films, books, games, and TV series that so marvelously explore the Dark Side. Regardless of whether or not we can ever accurately define or defeat the Dark Side, we are all indebted to the millions of people over the millennia who have taken a stand to hold the Light. May all of us be courageous enough to do so, in our lives and in our stories, now and in the future.

INTRODUCTION

Conflict lies at the heart of all effective stories.

Every good story requires three basic conflicts: the hero's internal flaw, an antagonist, and an external threat to the hero. These all need to be appropriate, balanced, believable, and capable of contributing to a satisfactory resolution. Ineffectiveness in these elements of conflict is one of the biggest problems storytellers have. That ineffectiveness can be the result of many things:

- from naiveté (it's all good) to cynicism (it's all bad)
- from making it too hard on the hero to not hard enough
- from an ineffective antagonist to one who overpowers the story
- from letting your message overpower the story to having no message at all
- from inappropriately mixing one's personal problems with the hero's to a lack of any believable human relevance
- from focusing on the hero's personal conflict to the exclusion of its universality, or vise versa
- plus many more individually unique barriers to building great conflict

There are two essential qualities of good stories: familiarity and surprise. The clever writer will use universally familiar concepts and principles (mythic themes, archetypes, and imagery) and give them a unique, surprising spin to entertain and enlighten us anew with the universal truths around which wonder and recognition circle in delight.

Three must-have aspects of good stories are sympathy, danger, and salvation. We must have sympathy for and interest in the protagonist; the protagonist must be placed in danger; there must be some sort of salvation, direct or implied, for a satisfactory (not necessarily happy) resolution.

You must never make it easy for your protagonist. Barriers, setbacks, detours, and delays are the stuff of drama. Selecting and developing effective conflict requires knowledge of the so-called Dark Side – all that which stands in the way of their desires and fulfillment.

To assist you in crafting your stories, this book will:

- Examine various perspectives on Evil and the Dark Side to widen and deepen your choices for selecting and creating characters and their conflicts
- Define the Three Levels of the Dark Side: what they are, how they work, and how to create characters and situations with them
- Examine Antagonists: antiheroes, evil-doers, seducers, bumblers, vampires, ghosts, aliens, etc. so you can more fully and believably develop those characters
- Investigate the Lure of the Dark Side, so your plots and actions are organic to your characters and stories
- Explore options your protagonist can use to confront, counteract, and defeat the Dark Side
- Suggest story tools for using all this information

But I'm writing a comedy, romance, children's fantasy, or documentary...

Since conflict is the very heart of story, these principles apply in any style, any genre.

The Dark Side is there in comedies: Dr. Evil and Mini-Me in *Austin Powers,* Cold War cartoon spies Boris and Natasha in the *Bullwinkle* TV series, and Cruella DeVil of Dalmation deviousness. Evil may not always pay, but sometimes it can be awfully funny.

Stories most popular with children have some seriously evil villains and deadly dangerous situations: *Harry Potter*, Grimm's Fairy Tales, *Star Wars*. Developing young minds require a sense of meaning, self importance, and optimism; the way heroes in these stories deal with the Dark Side offers insight and encouragement for the dangers inherent in any child's existence.

In romance stories the Dark Side is whatever comes between lovers, be it family feuds in *Romeo and Juliet*, 19th-century English societal barriers in *Pride and Prejudice*, or selfish indecisiveness in *My Best Friend's Wedding*.

Documentaries are only interesting and effective if there is an us-against-them element. Whether "them" is the environment, a bureaucracy, a disease, or a situation, you will only engage our interest and stir our actions if you show us conflict and choices.

Fairy tales, comedy, romantic comedy, black comedy, drama, action-adventure, horror, tragedy, historical fiction, documentaries... all need worthy opponents, dangers to heroines, and the opportunity for your audience to observe and experience transformation as the story moves through conflict to resolution. No matter the medium — from a theatrical blockbuster to a YouTube short, a massively multiplayer online game, or a torrid romance novel — without vivid and believable antagonists and threatening situations, there can be no heroics (whether of the heart or the sword), and hence no real story.

CONCLUSION

Conflict is the very heart and soul of drama, and the Dark Side offers worlds of conflict. Enjoy the exploration, add your own insights along the way to enhance the information, and use the suggestions to strengthen and expand your own skills and experience.

Put *The Power of the Dark Side* to work on your side to write and create Great Villains, Dangerous Situations, and Dramatic Conflicts to entertain and enlighten us all!

CAVEAT SCRIPTOR
= WRITER BEWARE

Can writing or playing a bad guy turn you into one? Can song lyrics cause suicide? Can working on a horror movie curse your real life? Maybe....

Storytellers create characters and situations from the sublime to the scary, the silly to the sleazy. Many of us find that our real lives imitate the stories we are working on, and vice versa. In *Wes Craven's New Nightmare,* evil-incarnate Freddy Krueger enters the real world through the filmmakers' dreams and emotions. Once a thing is seen as cursed, that feeling seems to bring about its own fulfillment; watch theater actors shiver when you mention "The Scottish Play" (Macbeth). Sophisticated philosophies have always taught that our perceptions influence our individual experience of reality, though not necessarily actual reality. If your perceptions are filled with Evil and the Dark Side while you're working on a project, it's fairly typical that some of that will spill over into your real life. How does that happen? What can you do to maintain a higher perspective and healthy balance?

Every thing that exists has a unique character, essence, or "is-ness", whether rock, flower, animal, person, family, company, story genre, situation, or concept such as democracy, love, or evil. Hindu teachings call this essence, or identity, a *deva* and the concept is everywhere, from rose-ness to cat-ness and more. The military has *esprit de corps,* French for "spirit of the body". *Zeitgeist* is German for "spirit of the time." Business has institutional memory and religions have dogma. Lovers have relationships, Jung labeled personalized universal qualities archetypes, and wars are fought over ideologies.

Devas influence us according to our receptiveness: the disaffected do not thrill to the national anthem, the disillusioned lover is immune to pleas and kisses, the non-believer pooh-poohs angels and aliens. Plug into a *deva*, however, and your life changes: religious converts, new lovers, revolutionaries, and avid fans are all affected by *devas*. Since consciousness is both radiatory and magnetic, put out a particular "vibe" and you'll attract that joy, cynicism, fear, etc. As my Texas grandmother used to tell us, "What you think about, you bring about."

You must make your story emotionally strong and compelling for your audience. If you aren't much affected by the relationship between you and your story, perhaps it isn't strong enough yet. But you don't want to be so swept up in it that you're immobilized by your own emotions, as well as your story's *devas*. Once I was reading a book about alien abductions that was so spooky I had to put it in the freezer at night so I could get to sleep. That's a very strong *deva*!

Storytellers have thin veils between their own souls and the rest of reality. That's what makes them so valuable — they can be a mirror and a movie screen for the rest of humanity, who have a curiosity for variety and adventure but often not the inclination, time, or courage to go there themselves.

The Hero's Journey involves a descent to the underworld, a battling with the forces of darkness, and a return with a boon for the community. Jesus harrowed Hell, sending the righteous to Heaven; Greek heroes Aeneas and Ulysses visited the scary bits of the underworld and gained support for their journeys; in *The Lord of the Rings*, Gandalf returned from his fall into the fiery abyss a stronger Wizard. All came back transformed with new insights and information to aid themselves and others. You can do this too, from your own descent into the shadow world of your stories.

One tenet in spiritual training is about range. The higher you ascend, the deeper you descend. Once you've seen the light on some situation, what better to do with it than take it down into the darkness where it's needed. Most of us wouldn't voluntarily do that, so life often conspires to send us there anyway. See what is drawn to you, and remember that that is what needs to be harrowed out, transformed, and released. Your privilege and your duty as storytellers is to do that for the rest of us, too, through the heroes and heroines you create.

Chapter 12, "Confronting the Dark Side," has many suggestions for you and your characters.

~1~

Defining The Dark Side

Before we use the Dark Side in our stories we need to understand it as well as possible so we don't create silly stereotypes or laughable situations, but rather great depth and effectiveness, regardless of genre or style. Because we write for the entire world these days, we need to be aware of diverse perspectives and experiences even as we reach towards the universal truths inside each one. ～

1.
WHAT DARK SIDE?

+ **What is Evil?**

+ **Who is Evil?**

+ **Why is there Evil?**

+ **What does Evil want?**

+ **Why is Evil sometimes so alluring?**

+ **What's the difference between Evil and Bad?**

+ **What can we learn from Evil?**

+ **How do we defeat/defuse Evil?**

Your characters will be richer if you know and include their world-view of Evil, its origins, its goals, and its methods, since these beliefs will color how they approach every aspect of the emotions and actions in the story. Dramatic conflict can be enhanced by bringing different characters' belief systems against each other, as well as taking a character through an arc from one belief to another, or to/from, from/to lack of belief.

WHAT IS EVIL?

IT DEPENDS WHO YOU ASK

Take death. Christianity calls death the wages of sin, a punishment. Buddhists see it as release from earthly suffering. Hindus deify death in the god Shiva, a natural part of the cycle of life. Simba's dad in *The Lion King* took a similar stance from the lion's point of view; no doubt the gazelles were not so sanguine about their place on the food chain. Assisted suicide is murder to some and sweet release to others. Some insist evil is just a perception; others insist pure Evil exists.

IT DEPENDS ON YOUR PERSPECTIVE

Military strategy often calls for a surgical strike to remove a growing problem. Eliminate one person or small group, the theory goes, and save hundreds or thousands. Would killing Hitler early on have been a good thing? Most would say yes. Yet we debate dropping atomic bombs on Japan to end war in the Pacific.

Tough love probably feels pretty evil to the person on the receiving end of it, such as teenagers struggling with parents over discipline-and-safety versus exploration-and-self-definition.

Pride and Prejudice makes clear the Bennett girls must battle not only a confining social structure where people of higher class barely recognize the existence of others, but also a silly mother. We find the social structure outdated, but we understand that those characters are bound within it.

Characters in the movie *Underworld: Evolution,* which pits vampires against werewolves, is full of judgment and justifications that vary greatly from side to side, though humans consider them all evil.

IN YOUR CREATIONS

The most interesting stories are those that lift the veils of convention and turn perspective around. As you build the world your heroine lives in, be sure to give clear indications of what people in her world consider good and bad. We need some idea of who's against who and why, though of course we want you to throw us off, toss up surprises, and offer new insights.

Who is Evil?

It Depends on Who's Deciding

Some traditions say the battle between Lucifer and the Archangel Michael was the battle between intellect and emotion. Emotion won and humans have been manipulated by it ever since. Lucifer, which means "light-bringer" in Latin, brings critical-thinking skills: the ability to assess situations and motives, foresee consequences, and make informed decisions. Faith is an emotion that takes the place of knowledge and is a powerful tool to control the unthinking masses.

Oppressive societies control communications, burn books, close schools, and kill intellectuals. If people lack information and critical-thinking skills, you can better control them through fear.

Fundamentalists of all stripes see "other" as evil.

Catholicism says seven years old is the age of accountability, so that's when you do your first Confession and Holy Communion. Supposedly you then understand right from wrong on a higher conceptual level than just the instinctual punishment-or-reward behavioral programming a kid gets. Dog-owners swear their animals can look furtively around before they do something "wrong," and then look whiningly guilty when caught. Then again, a one-year-old dog is equivalent to a seven year old child....

The charming animated film *Curse of the Were-Rabbit* has a slant on evil similar to that of many of the mystery systems, such as Mithraism and Masonry. When Wallace is warned "Beware the beast within," the nature of the beast is revealed when he looks in a mirror and sees... himself.

Some think no one does anything unless they believe they'll get some good from others, from some deity, or from themselves via self-righteousness. Others think when we're doing wrong, we know darn well it's wrong, but do it anyway. Then the "good" faction says we do wrong to get our good. Maybe. Yet sometimes you know you're hurting someone but you don't stop, you just keep feeding that dark/guilty/shameful maw inside yourself. Then the "good" faction says, "See, you were getting something you wanted — you wanted to feel awful." About then I throw my hands up and exit that debate.

At one end of the sliding scale of guilt is the person who simply does not have the brain wiring to feel shame or remorse. In *Se7en,* serial killer Kevin Spacey thinks he's performing a service to humanity by displaying the horrors of our sins. These people are called psychopaths. At the other end is the overly guilty, no-boundaries person who assumes blame for everything from the weather, to the food, to the state of the world. These people are called codependent.

Then there are somewhat bad people who kill evil people to save others, like the scruffy Catholic twins in *Boondock Saints* assassinating murderous Mafia guys, or outlaw Vin Diesel slaying evil necromongers out to take over the universe in *Chronicles of Riddick.*

IT DEPENDS ON TIME AND PLACE

In the conservative American '50s and '60s movies with wicked children, such as *The Bad Seed* and *Village of the Damned,* were horrifying because evil was embodied in children. Now it's no shocker for kids to be blood-sucking, murderous, evil demons. In stories, that is; we'd still like them to behave in restaurants and - theaters.

Women who smoke, wear pants, or speak their minds are considered scandalous in repressive times, like Victorian England and many contemporary cultures. Rebellious, pot-smoking, bra-burners of the 1960s became the gray-haired heroines of the later Feminist Movement, but girls of the 2000s hardly acknowledge them.

In some cultures a girl who even holds hands with a man can still be slain by her family for dishonoring them. Yet among the Tuareg of North Africa, unmarried girls are expected to have as much sex as possible with as many men as possible and to prove their fertility *before* marriage.

Cultural definitions of evil and impropriety vary so much as to be puzzling, if not downright comical. An Internet search for "silly laws" reveals it's illegal in Thailand to leave the house without underwear, in Sweden prostitution is legal but it is not legal to avail oneself of a prostitute's services, donkeys can't sleep in bathtubs in Arizona, and sex with animals is forbidden in Texas.

American soldiers flying over Mogadishu in helicopters offended Muslims because their legs were hanging out the sides of the choppers and they were "showing the soles of their feet," a supreme insult in that culture. The *Black Hawk Down* movie didn't mention this, but it's thought to have been an emotional trigger for that anti-American backlash.

IN YOUR CREATIONS

The more specifically and strongly you define Evil for the different characters in your story's situation, the more you heighten dramatic conflict. The sliding scale concept is an essential aspect of the character arc, transformation, and resolution.

WHY IS THERE EVIL?

Does it matter where evil comes from? For your characters, yes, it does, because their beliefs will influence their motivations and actions. People who believe in an afterlife may be much more willing to sacrifice themselves than people who think it's this life and this life only. People who base their actions on expected rewards or punishment from a Higher Being may be willing to break laws and make sacrifices in the here and now.

According to Duality theories, good and evil, light and dark continually battle for dominance, with one or the other destined to win. Both Judeo-Christianity and Islam posit an eventual victory by good over evil, so there's an inherent optimism even as believers suffer, become martyrs or murderers. Arthurian tales and stories of the Crusades, such as *Kingdom of Heaven*, reflect this view, as both Christian Crusaders and the Muslims they fought believed God/Allah would bring them victory.

The Teutonic system of northern Europe foretells Ragnarok, the dissolution of all things; yet it instills a sense of honor that encourages fighting against the inevitable. Richard Wagner's *Ring Cycle* operas about the fall of the Norse gods, and *Star Trek*'s gloomy Klingons embody this pessimistic but valiant philosophy.

In Unity theories "It's all good," and seeming duality is merely *maya* (illusion). Opposites arise mutually and cannot exist without each other. Rising above duality places one above conflict and is said to bring comfort, peace, and ultimately *nirvana* (total impersonal bliss). The round yin/yang symbol of Taoism illustrates the concept with intertwined dark and light tear shapes, each containing a spot of the other.

Yet both Duality and Unity beg an explanation as to why there is evil. Here are some.

SOMEBODY REBELLED

Judeo-Christianity posits a war in heaven between Yahweh and Lucifer. John Milton's *Paradise Lost* and William Blake's art and poetry richly recount this story.

A tale from mystic Islam relates a disillusioned Lucifer departing because God reneged on his initial agreement to always put angels first. Other Islamic traditions pose the deceiver Iblis (similar to Christian Satan) against the will of Allah.

The Siberian Tunga people's devil is Buninka, who challenges God. African Bushmen have Kaang the good creator versus Gauna who brings evil and trouble.

Even this duality of rebellion is reconciled in some mythologies into a unity. The Zoroastrian mythology of ancient Persia says that Ahura-Mazda the good allows Ahriman the evil to express itself, then eventually be conquered by good.

SOMEBODY GOOFED

A popular New Age explanation for how the world got this wonky is that our predecessors, the Atlanteans, were so technologically advanced they got too big for their britches, used crystal powers unwisely, and set off tectonic shifts that sank the continent. Some escaped to carry on secret teachings in the spirituality of the Egyptians, Celts, and Mesoamericans. This theory has echoes in Plato, Ignatius Donnely's *Atlantis*, and Madame Blavatsky's *The Secret Doctrine*.

Some Hindu Vedic stories recount that earthlings had sponsors from Venus helping us out during the Atlantean era, but after pride led to our downfall they gave up on us, left the planet in disgust, and put up a "Quarantine" sign. Supposedly, the quarantine was lifted once we exploded the first atomic bomb, and now beings from other worlds are once again visiting earth. Whether or not this is good or bad depends on whether you're watching *X-Files*, *Alien Nation*, or *Men in Black*, all of which deal in different ways with extraterrestrials.

IT'S ALL A SETUP

Greek myths have a curious woman unable to resist opening a forbidden box and releasing all the ills of the world. Thank goodness there was one thing left in Pandora's Box — Hope.

Some thinkers observe that Yahweh used reverse psychology on Eve and Adam because he knew if he told them to study and go to the school of life, they'd cut class and refuse to do their homework. Like Mark Twain's cunning boy in *Tom Sawyer,* who made others pay to paint the fence for him, Yahweh let the Serpent beguile Eve into showing some initiative and taking the path of Knowledge instead of just hanging around Paradise on an eternal vacation. The Persian poet Omar Khayyam, a Sufi mystic, has a rather cynical view of this setup and refuses to take the blame for his own inclinations and actions:

> Oh, Thou, who didst with Pitfall and with Gin
> Beset the Road I was to wander in,
>   Thou wilt not with Predestination round
> Enmesh me, and impute my Fall to Sin?

Or in plainer English, "Hey, God created both my appetites and martinis, so how is it my fault if I drink them?"

IT'S ALL A GAME

Those marvelous last scenes in the *Men in Black* movies show our galaxy and many others as just pieces in a vast game of marbles. Sufi poet Khayyam again offers an opinion:

> 'Tis all a Chequer-board of Nights and Days
> Where Destiny with Men for Pieces plays:
>   Hither and thither moves, and mates, and slays,
> And one by one back in the Closet lays.

Note the resemblance to Shakespeare's *As You Like It*:

> All the world's a stage,
> And all the men and women merely players:
> They have their exits and their entrances;
> And one man in his time plays many parts

IT'S ALL A CLASSROOM

Some think the existence of the Dark Side is like weights at the gym: there to help build spiritual muscles. Some reincarnationists see Evil as Karma, simply the balancing out of one action with another. You persecute others in one lifetime; you will be persecuted in another.

Earth as a primary prep school for the more sacred planets is part of some lore. In a few others, this is a rehab or prison planet... which would explain a lot, actually.

IT'S NOT OUR FAULT

Author Zecharia Sitchen interpreted as true the ancient Sumerian myths about the Anunaki, extraterrestrials who came to earth looking for resources and slaves. They performed genetic engineering on proto-human simians, created modern people, and put us to work in mines. *Stargate* the movie and TV series, as well as the popular cyber-punk novel *Snow Crash,* take off on this.

Scientology tells about ancient entities from other planets sent to earth for punishment, who attach to humans and cause all sorts of problems.

Julian May's *Many-Colored Land* quartet has aliens crashing here during the Pleistocene Era and becoming the early gods, who interact with humans from the modern era using a time machine to interact with... well, they're wonderfully complex novels.

In another time-twisting approach, *The Hitchhiker's Guide to the Galaxy* blames it on an elegant science experiment conducted on our planet by white rats, foiled by bureaucracy.

IT'S ALL OUR FAULT

Manichaean dualism deals with light trapped in matter, the Greek Orphic mystery religion stresses duality within the individual, and Swahili thought views us as a combination of good and evil, matter and spirit.

The angel Gabriel is said to have removed the *Haab* (dark spot) from Mohammed's heart. The Wisdom Schools teach that there's a dark spot within the heart of everything. Joseph Conrad's novel *Heart of Darkness* and Francis Ford Coppola's film *Apocalypse Now* explore this concept within individuals.

Anthropologists, evolutionary psychologists, and the slightly cynical might simply note our animal nature or reptilian brains, complete with cutthroat competition and oppressive hierarchies.

IT'S NOBODY'S FAULT

It's just the way things are. Nobody made it, nobody went bad, nobody goofed. This is reality. Accept it. Work with it.

For an amusing explanation of why there is evil, web search "shit happens."

IN YOUR CREATIONS

Dramatic conflict can be heightened by giving different characters conflicting philosophical interpretations: choose one for Character A and a different one for Character B, combine, then stand back. Or take a character from one belief system to another and watch their actions shift. In *The Matrix*, Keanu Reeves' Neo goes through a major transformation as he wakes up to reality and shifts from fighting boredom to fighting evil machines and bad people.

Based on natural selection so far, what might the next 65 million years look like? Will humans, like dolphins and whales, throw up our hands, give up so-called civilization, and go back to the sea to splash about, sing, and have lots of sex? Club Med thinks so.

WHAT DOES EVIL WANT?

Bwa-ha-ha-ha — world domination! Or, maybe not.

MAYBE IT WANTS TO TEACH US

Mythic systems feature monsters, demons, and seductive evils, both real and symbolic. Wise observers say it's to get us to explore and redeem the darkness within ourselves.

Greek tragedies dramatically portray the down side of going to the Dark Side. Because he accidentally married his own mother, Oedipus teaches us to do an Internet search on your dates before you get intimate (*Looking for Mister Goodbar, Body Heat, Fatal Attraction*). Singer and string player Orpheus was torn to bits by Maenads, girls gone wild; he teaches performers to leave the stage while you're still on top, before all goes bad and the fans tear you apart (*Performance, The Doors, Almost Famous, Still Crazy*).

In the Old Testament, Satan (Hebrew for "adversary") was often working with/for Yahweh, testing humans like Job.

The fable about Midas's golden touch and the movie *Wall Street* show the wages of greed, while Shakespeare's *Julius Caesar* and the HBO series *Rome* reveal how power corrupts. The background conflict in the TV series *Babylon 5* is over the best way for the old races to spur evolution of younger races: "Conflict!" urge the vicious Shadows, or "Support!" offer the benevolent Vorlons.

MAYBE IT WANTS TO PROTECT US

Evil is just a good that's been held onto too long, or so the Ageless Wisdom tells us. Some racism may be an aversion to outsiders who carry deadly germs, as with the decimation of Pacific Islanders by European colonists' diseases. Science has revealed that this aversion to "other" is hardwired into our brains.

Psychologists note how defense mechanisms of our youth become neurosis in our adulthood, as in *Postcards from the Edge* where Carrie Fisher strives for recognition beneath her movie star mom's shadow. Grown-up wounds cause scabby characteristics, like Jane

Austin's gloomy Mister Darcy in *Pride and Prejudice,* and Ayn Rand's hyper-individualistic heroes in *Atlas Shrugged.*

MAYBE IT WANTS ITS OWN REDEMPTION

Deathbed conversions are familiar stories. Darth Vader finally reaches out to his son Luke Skywalker in *Return of the Jedi.* Colonel Kurtz, who realizes he's gone way over the edge of sanity and forgiveness, encourages Captain Willard to sacrifice him in *Apocalypse Now.*

MAYBE IT WANTS POWER, SELF-AGGRANDIZEMENT, REVENGE

Natural Born Killers (murderous kids and ravenous media), *Hotel Rwanda* (ethnic hatreds), the *Godfather* trilogy (mob rivalries), and *The Lord of the Rings* (power struggles for empire) explore these aspects of the Dark Side on a rampage.

MAYBE IT JUST WANTS DESTRUCTION

In *Wes Craven's New Nightmare,* writer/director/star Craven explains Freddie Kreuger as the embodiment of an ancient evil that thrives on the death of innocents. In *Schindler's List,* Nazi Ralph Fiennes admits he's in thrall to the destruction of his tormenting desire for a Jewish woman.

IN YOUR CREATIONS

Whatever it wants, Evil is powerful and undeniable. You need to know the ultimate goal of your Evil people, events, and situations, since that will determine both motivations and actions in your story. Your antagonists will fight for it; your protagonist against it. It can also provide surprises and resolutions as you reveal the deeper meanings behind characters' actions.

WHY IS EVIL SOMETIMES SO ALLURING?

The nature of life is growth, expansion, exploration. To fit into society we must curb our natural impulse towards total expansion of Self and the indulgence of all our desires. People or situations who throw off these constraints are intriguing because they manifest our deepest drives. The eternal battle between Self and Others is the conundrum of civilization. When do we demand our due? When do we sacrifice for others? The allure of Evil may well be the allure of doing just as we desire, without having to consider anyone else's well being.

A great example is Ian Richardson playing unscrupulous Francis Urquhart in the BBC miniseries *House of Cards, To Play the King,* and *The Final Cut.* We see Urquhart's villainy at the very beginning, yet as he breaks the fourth wall and comments to us, we are drawn into his Machiavellian manipulations, and we watch with fascinated horror as he uses other people's faults and foibles to hoist them on their own petards.

Also, there's no doubt we have a morbid fascination with destruction. Maybe it's instinct. Maybe it's perversity. Maybe it's an inherent disassociation of our soul from our body. Witness lookie-loo slowdowns for highway crashes and the sexual aberration focused on car accidents explored in J.G. Ballard's book and David Cronenberg's movie *Crash.*

Then there's awe of the sublime, our fascination with the mystery and sheer beauty of power, be it a raging storm or a pouncing tiger. We respond in different ways: freeze like deer in headlights (Clarice in *The Silence of the Lambs*), challenge it (*The Perfect Storm*), submit like weaker dogs to an alpha (Ian McShane and Powers Booth's alpha-male characters in the HBO series *Deadwood*), or take power up and wield it over others (Aragorn and Gandalf in *The Lord of the Rings*).

We desire to test our mettle, and what better way than against the truly worthy opponent. What's the value of fighting a small thing? Going up against the really big bad guys brings much more glory. Clarice going up against Hannibal Lecter in *The Silence of the Lambs* takes a lot of courage, and it makes her a heroine.

IN YOUR CREATIONS

Be clear what aspect attracts your character. Show us the ups and downs. Reveal the attraction in small bits, beginning with curiosity, moving to fascinating, then to sign-on, and ultimately to satisfaction or sorrow.

WHAT'S THE DIFFERENCE BETWEEN EVIL AND BAD?

Motivation. Or the lack thereof. Evil has intent to harm. Bad is simply the opposite of good, a bit of antisocial rebellion. It's the difference between bunko squad and homicide. It's misdemeanors versus felonies.

Danny, Rizzo, and Kenickie in *Grease* are bad; Marlon Brando and Lee Marvin in *The Wild One* ride towards evil. In *Pitch Black* and *The Chronicles of Riddick*, outlaw Vin Diesel is a bad man — and the only one who can stop the really evil guys. The vigilante twins of *Boondock Saints* may be bad, but they're not evil. They're balancing the indifference of good men towards evil men.

Philadelphia is about a bad impersonal disease (AIDS); *Angels in America* is about the evil tendency to ignore that disease and punish the victims.

In *Armeggedon*, Bruce Willis battles a rock. The rock has no intent – it's not evil, it's just really bad for us. The alien antagonists of *Independence Day* have evil intentions of taking over earth. In both cases it's a bunch of deadheads who save us, led by Willis in *Armeggedon* and Randy Quaid in *Independence Day*.

IN YOUR CREATIONS

It's all about motivation. Have characters discover the difference through the course of the story. In *Double Indemnity* and *Body Heat,* the men think the women are just bad, but they're really evil. Conversely, when the supposedly evil turns out to be simply bad, typical dialogue goes, "I was wrong about you," as in *Road Warrior* when the refuges discover Mad Max isn't one of the evil marauders. In *Boondock Saints*, the discovery is an hilarious scene with Willem Dafoe in a Catholic confessional.

WHAT CAN WE LEARN FROM EVIL?

What not to do. Or if you're leaning towards the Dark Side, some good tips.

By confronting Evil we learn our strengths and weaknesses. We learn what counts. We learn our prejudices and the weaknesses in our systems and defenses. In psychology as in physics, stress will occur at the point of least resistance, offering instant analysis on what needs fixing.

Tragedies offer catharsis and instruction. German philosopher Friedrich Nietszche advises, "That which does not kill us makes us stronger." Would we condemn the fire that tempers the steel? Without it there is no sword.

IN YOUR CREATIONS

Craft your story such that your heroine is challenged both within and without, so your audience can be enlightened and informed in a similar way.

Whatever Evil or Dark Side your characters face, be sure they learn some lesson and that both they and we get it, even if they don't apply it in this story.

HOW DO WE DEFEAT/ DEFUSE EVIL?

Various answers have impelled people to toss virgins into volcanoes, wear hair shirts, and crawl cruel miles on their hands and knees. Others have been impelled to shrug at the seeming injustice of existence, then set about bettering the world.

Just as many mythologies have Teacher Gods, they also have Protector Gods. Artemis/Diana protected Greco-Roman mothers during childbirth. Resurrecting Saviour Gods — Egyptian Osiris, Mesopotamian Dammuz, Norse Baldur, and Christian Jesus — are often called upon as protectors from evil and death. The Asian goddess Kwan Yin protects homes, and Catholic Saint Christopher protects travelers.

IN YOUR CREATIONS

In Chapter 12, "Confronting the Dark Side," there are many more suggestions that vary according to the nature of the Evil, the abilities of your protagonist, and the tools at hand.

CONCLUSION

It is fatally naïve to believe there is no real danger, no Dark Side, no evil in humanity and the world. Most of our energies are dedicated to holding back the tide of Darkness, be it battling our own flaws, those who wish us harm, fighting disease, struggling against the elements, or resisting the march of time. How we approach this endless challenge molds our stories and our very lives. The seemingly eternal conflict between good and evil, the light and the dark, is what makes good stories. Your conscious use of varying attitudes and approaches to this conflict can make great stories.

∼II∼

THE THREE
LEVELS OF THE
DARK SIDE

Just because you're paranoid doesn't mean they aren't after you, but it may not be Darth Vader himself causing you all that trouble.

Common sense as well as the Ageless Wisdom divides the Dark Side into three aspects: personal, impersonal, and supra-personal. It's the classic paradigm of only three storylines: man against man, man against nature, man against the gods. ∼

2.
THE DWELLER ON
THE THRESHOLD -
PERSONAL

✦ **Our own Shadow**

✦ **Illness, wounds, and death**

✦ **When bad things happen to silly people**

✦ **Dark night of the Soul**

✦ **Gang-related**

✦ **Karma**

Can't finish that script? Don't have the relationship you want? Others don't appreciate your genius? Too often we blame our failures on the indifference or wrath of the gods or the evil actions of the Dark Ones. Most often though, it's just us getting in our own way. The Devil Tarot Card shows a naked man and woman chained to a block upon which crouches a devil. Their chains are loose — the bondage is of their own making. It's more the Dim Side than the Dark Side. Then there are illnesses, phobias, stupidity, social ills, and spiritual dilemmas... all hold us back.

These internal glitches are called "The Dweller on the Threshold." Whatever its source or manifestation, the Dweller blocks the doorway to our dreams. The Ageless Wisdom says the only way to move through the doorway is to "become the doorway." Once your character admits the problem and deals with it, they can move on.

Indiana Jones conquered his snake phobia in *Raiders of the Lost Ark* and saved the day. Alan Rickman's Dr. Lazarus softened his arrogance in *Galaxy Quest* to give a dying young alien, and himself, the gift of true acceptance.

Here are some major Dwellers that block our Thresholds.

OUR OWN SHADOW

Cynicism, laziness, petulance, procrastination, phobias, arrogance, entitlement, obsessions, guilt, etc.: Our core wounds and fatal flaws are triggers for drama. They foil our plans, hold us back, and like a wicked magnet, seem to draw misfortune down upon us.

Reincarnationists say our foibles are the blowback of deeds from other lifetimes. Other religions blame our own tendencies and/or supernatural temptation and persecution. Psychologists look to early experiences and unconscious desires. Astrologists talk about being born under a bad sign. Psychiatrist Carl Jung called unacknowledged and unexpressed parts of our selves our Shadow. Mythologist Joseph Campbell pointed out the parallel psychological symbolism of Threshold Guardians in Hero's Journey myths.

Passionate obsession blinds us to propriety, as in *Fatal Attraction,* with adultery and death; and to higher duty, as in the illicit love between Lancelot and Guinevere that shatters Camelot. Jealousy and envy drive some to madness, like weasely Gollum and his "precious" in *The Lord of the Rings. Schadenfreud* (delight in another's misfortune) sells lots of tabloids and reality TV. Troubled adolescents offer plenty of dramatic Shadow stuff: *28 days, Girl Interrupted, My Own Private Idaho, American Beauty.* Fear of success or failure — *A Star is Born, Sunset Boulevard, The Doors,* and many stories about performers deal with these Shadows.

Grief is a process and guilt a signpost, neither are a destination. Yet, some kids feel they're at fault for their parents' divorce. Some parents feel a child's death is their fault, as in *Fearless,* where a mom loses her infant when she can't hold on tightly enough in a plane crash. Many are burdened by misplaced guilt over a sibling's death, as in *Ordinary People.*

Suicide is a major Dweller that has touched many families. Besides the tragic loss of a loved one, suicide can rob others of hope and infect them with despair.

A. IN ACTION

An entire industry helps people with their Shadows, from shrinks to self-help books.

Julius Caesar overestimated Rome's tolerance for his Imperial ambitions. Both Napoleon and Hitler overestimated their own powers against the Russian winter. Arrogance finds a perfect home in politics; just read history or watch the news.

The core meaning of *jihad* is an "internal struggle against evil." Many personal, familial, and societal conflicts are about people trying to impose their own Dwellers on others.

The victim culture of late 20th-century America exploits the Shadow: the Twinkie defense, Jerry Springer, reality TV, celebrity confessions, frivolous lawsuits, *ad nauseum.*

B. IN MEDIA

Petulance is not always petty. Achilles, Greek hero of *The Iliad* and the movie *Troy,* pouts in his tent over King Agamemnon's appropriating his hostage girl, Briseas. The warrior's three-day absence from the battlefield causes grave consequences, and only the death of Achilles' beloved cousin Patroclus gets him back into action again.

In *The Man Who Would Be King* pride and avarice lead to the downfall and death of Sean Connery's Danny. The Japanese film *In the Realm of the Senses* shows the tragic unraveling of sexual obsession. In *Big Fish* a remote son explores his father's foibles and discovers his own. In *Road to Perdition* two mob fathers love their flawed sons so much they cover up fatal mistakes.

The comedy *Free Enterprise* features William Shatner as himself doing a rap version of *Julius Caesar,* as the almost-thirty heroes come to terms with their death grip on youth.

Watch the opening sequence of *Apocalypse Now* where Captain Willard battles his Dweller. Crushed between desire to be back in the jungle and disgust at the killer he's become, Martin Sheen's Willard drinks to excess, fights himself in a mirror, and falls apart.

Judi Dench and Cate Blanchett in *Notes on a Scandal* prove the old saying that we are prisoners of our own desires. In *The Legend of 1900* Tim Roth is a prisoner of his own fear, a talented pianist stuck on the ocean liner where he was born, afraid to get off the boat and enter the real world.

Many games use the concept of our own foibles to create villains and drawbacks for players: *Xenogears* and *Xenosaga*.

C. IN YOUR CREATIONS

Inner Drives Center of Motivation - Lower Solar Plexus: personal identity and power, & Sacral: sexuality.

Internal problems can be the central conflict or the subplot conflict, occasionally both. In *Adaptation* the main character's internal conflict is also the story conflict.

For secondary and minor characters, internal flaws can enhance depth of personality. Just as we project our own faults onto others, so too can you personify your heroine's foibles in minor characters. How she interacts with them gives us clues to her internal self.

Have at least one strong personality foible per character. Give early hints about your character's problems, like Indiana Jones's fear of snakes and Carrie Fisher's drug dependence, both revealed in the first few minutes of *Raiders of the Lost Ark* and *Postcards from the Edge*.

Self-exploration may find the key to overcoming both your character's psychological problems and the larger story conflict, as in *The Long Kiss Goodnight* where Geena Davis emerges from amnesia to discover she's a superagent and actually can defeat her assassins. *The Bourne Identity* uses the same plot line. Watch *Fight Club* and *Training Day* for characters with interwoven inner/outer conflicts.

Check out the Seven Deadly Sins for more Dweller ideas: Pride, Envy, Anger, Laziness, Greed, Gluttony, Lust.

ILLNESSES, WOUNDS, & DEATHS

Illness and death seem so inherently wrong that we often blame it on disfavor of gods, demons, spirits, or the curses of other humans. Some old cultures sensed such inherent wrongness in defects that they allowed imperfect newborns to die, or like herds of animals, abandoned the old and the weak.

Eastern medicine views diseases holistically and takes into account both emotions and environment.

New Age thought offers disease as simply our own resistance to the inherent well-being of existence: there is no evil, just failure to recognize the good. This may be part of how spontaneous healings and psychic surgery work. But for it to last, you must stay consciously aware — not an easy task.

A. IN ACTION

One drawback of the create-your-own-reality theory is that if you're sick, it's your own fault, so heal yourself. Granted there are psychosomatic illnesses, but if it's unconscious (or a baby), then how are you at fault?

Think of all the writers and artists who are alcoholics, drug addicts, or otherwise hindered by a Dweller. Think of what they might have accomplished without that burden. Then again, some say that without the burden, there would not have been the doorway to the other world where creativity lives for them.

Science continues to leech all the romance out of madness and suggests our fascinating character flaws are just chemical imbalances. Romeo and Juliet are no longer star-crossed lovers, they're codependent. Heathcliff in *Wuthering Heights* is no longer a brooding melancholic madly in love with the wrong woman, he's a depressive. *Gypsy*'s Mama Rose is no longer just a stage mom, she's a serious case of mania. Some masochism and sadism have been found to have neurological bases: somehow the pain and pleasure wirings got crossed at an early age and these people truly can not feel one without the other.

B. IN MEDIA

Many myths are about finding the magic elixir to heal the wounded king (Amfortas in the Holy Grail stories) or bring immortality to the people (Gilgamesh). *Medicine Man, Lorenzo's Oil, The Constant Gardener,* and *The Fountain* reflect this mythic theme. So do Steve Martin in *Leap of Faith,* Ellen Burstyn in *Resurrection,* and the boy in *Carnivale,* all of whose special healing abilities cause problems.

The TV series *House* intelligently combines psychosomatic and physical ailments in plot and subplot to great dramatic effect, such as when a Shadow-side foible (infidelity) leads to an illness (STD). The TV series *Monk* makes light of a phobia; Howard Hughes in *The Aviator* suffers greatly from his.

Some of the most tragic stories are about addictions: *Leaving Las Vegas, Days of Wine and Roses, Sid and Nancy, When a Man Loves a Woman.* Some can also be funny: *Arthur, Postcards from the Edge, The Big Lebowski.*

Tales uplifting and tragic are told about people dealing with afflictions, or not, and what all of us can learn from them: *Forest Gump*, *Rainman*, *The Miracle Worker*.

Wounded characters can motivate others, as King Amfortas sets Parsifal on the Holy Grail trail (with echoes in *The Fisher King*), or drive the whole plot, as in *Phantom of the Opera* where a wounded man's twisted love brings the house down, literally.

Though few films are actually about the death process, death scenes are big deals for actors and can bring on tears. *Jacob's Ladder* shows one way to depart this world — just let go. *Ghost* also offers hints — make peace, with love. *The Sixth Sense* teaches release as well. Both the Egyptian and Tibetan *Book of the Dead* are great how-to-die guides.

C. IN YOUR CREATIONS

Inner Drives Center of Motivation - Various. The book details illnesses inherent to specific Centers.

A balance of inner and outer obstacles creates more interesting stories. Matching the illnesses and phobias to theme and plot increases richness. Director Alfred Hitchcock did this well with vertigo in *Vertigo* and in *Rear Window*, where a broken leg triggers dangerous voyeurism.

Live by the sword, die by the sword. Make your characters' illnesses, wounds, and deaths align with their personalities and actions. The arrogant, mercenary bad guys in *Die Hard 2* hijack a plane and an airport, killing hundreds of innocent people. They themselves die a fiery death in a plane crash.

Check out Eastern medicine correspondences of emotions to illnesses. Repressed rage = skin rashes, anger = liver problems, not speaking up = throat problems, etc.

WHEN BAD THINGS HAPPEN TO SILLY PEOPLE

Sometimes the Dweller sets up housekeeping in a really stupid place, like on a known fault line or flood plain. Having moved from Tornado Alley in Texas to Earthquake Central in LA, I can't criticize too much; but really, sometimes you just want to say, "What were you thinking?!"

We're not talking about innocents hoodwinked by unscrupulous developers into living atop old uranium mines, or health-seeking individuals believing the claims of unscrupulous doctors or pharmaceutical companies. This category is when people flaunt common sense and ignore obvious warnings — the Dark Brotherhood need waste no time on them, as they'll bring about their own demise.

A. IN ACTION

Science has identified an actual risk gene, not surprisingly found in people drawn to danger: skydiving, bungee jumping, extreme sports, and "Look — no hands!"

Developmental psychologists note that teenagers' disregard for danger is due in part to undeveloped brain regions that process risk assessment. They truly don't get how dangerous something might be.

People who should know better still do silly things, like help Madame Abacha from Nigeria transfer all that money out of the country, or they buy devices off the Internet to increase the size of their %*$&^.

B. IN MEDIA

Trickster gods like the Southwest American Indians' Coyote help expose silly peoples' idiocy by leading them on wild goose chases for riches, power, or lust.

Just think of all those stupid people in horror films who decide to go into that room that just ate their friends or split up and walk alone into the woods where five people just got mutilated.

Or how about people who pursue obviously bad romantic choices?

The heroes in most action-adventure movies, martial arts movies, Bond films, and a majority of games manage to escape all the dire consequences that would easily kill normal humans, but the ill-prepared bad guys usually die doing something they should know better than to even try.

Stupid comedies play off this tendency, be it the Three Stooges or the *Dumb and Dumber* guys. Sometimes they do best the so-called smarter guys, but mostly we laugh at this extreme portrayal of our own tendencies. Sitcoms are all about silly people telling fibs and evading responsibility.

C. IN YOUR CREATIONS

Inner Drives Center of Motivation - Root Center: lack of survival skills brings on silly actions and harmful, sometimes fatal, consequences.

The discovery of how stupid something is should be revealed to the audience before the character realizes it; that way we worry about them. Or if they're stupid, we wait with glee to watch them fall.

If you're doing a Lesson story, be sure to show the better way to do something: read labels, do soil samples, get second opinions, check references, etc.

If it's just a comedy, no worries. No one takes the *Road Runner* cartoons to task for not giving better life lessons... although we do learn not to order gizmos from ACME.

THE DARK NIGHT OF THE SOUL

Spiritual troubles plague believers when some event occurs to shake their faith. This cognitive dissonance can dissolve dogma and cause angry resentment towards the gods.

Wisdom Teachings call this the Dark Side of Initiation — when the loving aspirations and all-is-one-all-is-good feelings give way to the harsh reality of existence. Without guidance many are lost at this stage of the enlightenment game. Spiritual advisors can help one move beyond this deconstruction of unquestioning faith to find deeper anchorage in what mystics call the ineffable mystery of life and creation.

Not only religious people face this problem. The idealistic, the optimistic, the ambitious... anyone with a vision of "how it could/ should be" can be shattered. Selfish disappointments don't qualify; painful readjustments of entire worldviews do.

A. IN ACTION

Meditations and ancient practices help one past the logic barriers to a higher vision which accepts paradox. As the Buddhist saying goes:

1) first there is a mountain (our regular perception of reality),

2) then there is no mountain (that blissful spark of all-is-one awareness),

3) then there is (years of hard work to embody spiritual principles into regular reality).

Some say this Dark Night is what happened to the Peace Movement of the 1960s after the assassinations of John Kennedy, Robert Kennedy, and Martin Luther King Jr. Topped off by President Nixon's Watergate scandal, the disillusioned idealists retreated further into sex, drugs, and rock and roll and let the dreams die.

Others argue it just went underground and is resurfacing as retiring, empty-nest, former-hippie Baby Boomers get second wind.

"A cynic is just a wounded romantic" fits this pattern. Too many brilliant idealistic people get shot down by the ugly parts of humans and nature, then they spend the rest of their lives licking their wounded hearts while building up armor so that nothing can ever disappoint them again. Simon and Garfunkel's "I am a rock, I am an island" lyrics express this.

B. IN MEDIA

Some of our most beautiful art and poetry have been wrested from this Dark Night. In the 16th century, Spanish Carmelite St. John of the Cross wrote *The Dark Night of the Soul*, still relevant today for poignant longing and loneliness, as well as advice to others passing through this phase.

There's a moving speech in *The Lord of the Rings: The Two Towers* when Sam Gangee encourages Frodo to continue the quest to get the ring to Mount Doom. Sam refers to stories which insist there's something good in this world and it *is* worth fighting for.

Douglas Adams' sci-fi novel *The Long Dark Tea Time of the Soul* plays off this iconic phrase and concept. TV heroine Buffy has a number of Dark Night crises throughout the *Vampire Slayer* series, as do other humans, witches, and vampires. G'Kar in the TV series *Babylon 5* emerges from his Dark Night a better man; Ambassador Molari does not.

C. IN YOUR CREATIONS

Inner Drives Center of Motivation - Heart & Crown: Spiritual issues spring from and effect these higher centers.

Old Testament hero Jacob wrestles all night with an angel. Jacob wouldn't give up, demanded a blessing, and got it. Use this Dark

Night metaphor for your characters: they wrestle with a problem, are wounded, then using strength and stamina, gain benefit from the suffering. Like some recovery systems advise, it's only a mistake if you don't learn from it.

First establish your character's beliefs (see "What Dark Side?") and then proceed to shake them apart. Some people go back at a higher turn of the spiral, from literal to metaphorical interpretation of holy writ, perhaps. Others move on to casual agnosticism. Still others strike out in pain, while some retreat into darkness.

Have your disillusioned character expose human corruptions within the spiritual system. Have it parallel a similar problem within himself. Sexual and financial scandals are perfect examples.

Expand a character's beliefs from parochial (religious) to universal (spiritual) via a Dark Night.

GANG-RELATED

Peer pressure, mob psychology, the lemming instinct... it's bad enough having your own Dweller on the Threshold blocking your way. Worse yet is having a gang of them. Too many people are never given the chance to be individuals; many others are afraid to do so lest they incur the wrath of others or fail in their efforts. Our animal nature tends towards herding and hive mentality. Our human nature tends towards individuation. Our spiritual nature tends towards group consciousness: working for the greater good without sacrificing the self. The gang-related Dweller stops us from rising above the animal level.

A. IN ACTION

Exiled from cliques, wounded egos can strike back in school shootings. Gang wars, race riots, ethnic cleansing, and genocide are extremes of this Gang Dweller.

Though it's supposedly the next step in the evolution of human consciousness, shifting from tribalism or feudalism to a (somewhat) individualist system causes resistance and often bloodshed: Periclean Greece, unification of the Warring States in China, Renaissance Europe, the Age of Enlightenment, the Philippines' People Power revolution, and the attempted imposition of democracy in Iraq.

Failed revolutions can often be attributed to the Gang Dweller taking over. The 1790s French Revolution touted Liberty-Fraternity-Equality, but it resulted in a blood-drenched dictatorship and a return to feudal monarchy. The 1917 Russian Revolution slid almost immediately from feudal monarchy to gang-controlled pseudo-equality. See more under Latin American history and current events.

B. IN MEDIA

The core premise of the Hero's Journey is the individual separating from the tribe to create something new. *The Matrix* is an example of the individual (Neo) breaking out of the collective.

Other movies with this concept: *Incident at Owl Creek, Heathers, The Breakfast Club, Fight Club, Gangs of New York, Wild Things, Fountainhead, West Side Story, Colors, Boyz n the Hood, Evita, Les Miserables.*

TV series *Dawson's Creek* and *Buffy the Vampire Slayer* have teen characters dealing with this issue.

C. IN YOUR CREATIONS

Inner Drives Center of Motivation – Lower Solar Plexus: tribal consciousness and individualization, & Root: survival.

Clearly set up different goals and stakes for both individualism and the gang.

Show the upside of gangs: sense of community, belonging, support, fun; and the downside of individuation: loneliness, criticism, persecution, self doubt.

Give your heroine three runs at the problem and have her set back, or victorious, against 1) history's inertia, 2) the gang's agenda, 3) her own desire to belong.

Help discover tools to overcome this common problem. Offer us new perspectives on transformation and growth of consciousness.

See more in the "Groupthink Stinks" chapter.

KARMA, CULTURE, GENETIC MEMORY

Karma is a law of physics and a theory of metaphysics embraced by billions of humans. Physics is Newton's Third Law: For every action there is an opposite and equal reaction. Metaphysics? Certainly there are repercussions for our actions, both internal and external, short-term and long-term. Yet some good goes unrewarded and some evil unpunished. Karma attempts to explain these seeming inequities with a very long view of cause and effect.

Oppressed? You were the oppressor 300 years ago and it's payback time. A ruler? You learned to be a good one from many lifetimes suffering under bad ones. Broken heart? You broke hers last lifetime. Is Karma a Dweller? Just ask anyone who's a minority via skin, accent, etc. According to reincarnation, that's your problem because you chose to be born that way. Karma both unites us in the family of humanity and isolates us as captains of our own destiny.

Perhaps phobias such as arachnophobia, acrophobia, etc. are karmic species memories from the distant past when nature posed more danger. How they hold us back now makes for effective internal character obstacles. Some say we loathe lizards because of mammalian brain memories of dinosaur bullies... but paleobiology says that's a bit of a stretch. Good for sci-fi, though, like reptilian aliens in the 80s TV series *V* and *Alien Nation*.

A. IN ACTION

Responsible teachers warn students on the Spiritual Path they'll start drawing in Karma — their own, their family's, their culture's, etc., and they can expect illness, break ups, bankruptcies, even death as they consciously work on cleaning up and raising consciousness. Most disciplines prepare you for this, but it's always hard — though eventually worth it as the negative Karma gets worked out and the positive Karma comes through.

Psychiatry now deals with whole families and bloodlines. You may think you've escaped your family, but a trip back for a holiday or funeral will reveal others with your looks, your quirks, your tendencies. Scary.

Some illustrate Karma bounceback by reading Old Testament accounts about Israelites wiping out entire peoples, then read from Nazi Germany Holocaust accounts, then news from today's Israeli-Palestinian conflict. You could do exactly the same thing for just about any other group, ethnicity, or race. None of us are innocent if you go far enough back... sometimes only a year or two.

B. IN MEDIA

In both *Pride and Prejudice* and the Bollywood romp *Bride and Prejudice*, family and societal Karma provide obstacles to true love. Gabriel Garcia Marquez's novels also trace this, especially *One Hundred Years of Solitude*. Frank Herbert's *Dune* series deals with genetic memory, as does Paddy Chayefsky's *Altered States* where a scientist reverts back to a primate. *Star Trek: The Next Generation* did an episode where crew people turned into animals reflecting their races or personalities.

Though a staple of Eastern stories for thousands of years, Karma is just beginning to figure in Western stories long dominated by Judeo-Christian-Islamic views of only one earthly life. Karma is a plot driver in *Dead Again* and *The Fountain*. Mixing Christian and Eastern philosophies, *What Dreams May Come* portrays vivid Karmic results for taking one's own life.

C. IN YOUR CREATIONS

Inner Drives Center of Motivation – Root: Survival, & Lower Solar Plexus: separatism, tribalism. Sometimes Throat: attempted logic and balance, & occasionally Crown: higher spiritual forces.

Show us how the Karmic system works. What are the customs, the expectations, the limitations? In both *Pride and Prejudice* and *Bride and Prejudice* we are introduced to upper middle class wedding expectations; then we see what happens when customs and Karmic patterns are flaunted.

The Law of Grace supersedes the Law of Karma. Once you get the Lesson, you no longer have to pay the Karmic price. This tenet of the Wisdom Teachings is behind forgiveness, salvation, and the self sacrifice of all Redeemer Gods. Show how this works to free your character from the chains that once bound him.

Everything's moving so fast these days, it needn't take lifetimes to get payback. Show a heroine whose Karmic repercussions come ever more quickly until it's "instant Karma."

CONCLUSION

In order to change and grow, your characters must overcome inner obstacles, their Dwellers on the Threshold. Select a sliding scale, as between Loyalty and Obsession, and work your character along it. Too much reformation, however, leads to boring characters. In the TV series *House*, the Vicodin-addicted jerk Dr. House was without pain for a few episodes and became a nice guy... boring! The German philosopher Johann Goethe advised that you should beware when casting out your demons lest you cast out the best part of yourself.

Also keep in mind that how people view the Dwellers will affect their politics and policies. If it's your own fault you're homeless, you don't deserve assistance (conservatives). If it's cultural or societal, perhaps you do (liberals).

In *Jacob's Ladder* chiropractor and psychopomp (helpful guide to the underworld) Danny Aiello teaches dying soldier Tim Robbins that your Dwellers are demons until you let go of them. Then they are angels who take you towards the Light. English philosopher M. Jagger advises, "You can't always get what you want. But if you try sometimes, you just might find, you get what you need." Once we've learned what we needed to learn by battling our Dwellers, once we've stepped over our Dwellers, embraced them, become them, gone through them — we cross the Threshold into a totally different world.

3.
THE DARK FORCES
— IMPERSONAL

+ **Laws of physics**

+ **Theories of other physics**

+ **Time**

+ **Duality**

+ **Earth, Air, Fire, and Water**

+ **Red in tooth and claw**

+ **A plague on both your houses**

+ **Techno trouble**

In nature there are neither rewards nor punishments — there are only consequences. Whether fighting gravity to take flight, racing against time, hunting animals or escaping from them, battling diseases, or struggling to survive storms, humans thrill to stories of Us versus Nature. Unlike opposition from a Dweller on the Threshold, or from other intelligences, a Dark Force is a vastly different opponent. These impersonal Forces of Nature are only called Dark when they stand in opposition to our goals and desires. The Dark Forces can be especially frightening because there's no way to reason with them, yet they are the essence of physical reality and must be dealt with all the time.

Myths offer exciting personifications of Nature: volcano goddesses such as Hawaiian Pele of the fiery red hair, sea gods such as Greek

Poseidon, and the fierce jaguar gods of South America. Ingmar Bergman's somber film *The Seventh Seal* portrays the Grim Reaper as a dark-clad, chess-playing humanoid during the Black Plague. In Terry Pratchet's highly amusing *Discworld* fantasy books, Death is an overworked executive who outsources his professional duties and worries excessively about his rebellious teenage daughter.

Though not as glamorous as the angry gods of myth and legend, impersonal Dark Force dangers can push along a story quite well. In *Finding Nemo* many of the bad things are just doing what they do: big fish eat little fish, jellyfish sting anything in their way. In *The Perfect Storm,* the men's personal (Dweller) foibles get them into the storm, but they're battling an impersonal Dark Force, not an angry sea god.

Though prayer may comfort the devotee, it's not proven to affect objective reality and would seem neutralized where different people are praying or sacrificing for opposing results. Perhaps for this very reason, some of our greatest heroes and villains are those who control the Dark Forces, be it Gandalf or Sauron in *The Lord of the Rings*, Obi Wan or Darth Vader in *Star Wars*, Merlin, Moses, shamans, witches, or Harry Potter.

Dark Forces gone rogue supply the antagonist in many horror stories, be it hungry trees, killer bees, or raging storms.

Even if your story is totally realistic and centered on human interaction, you'll still want some aspect of the Dark Forces in play: the ticking clock, the physical obstacle, faulty technology, etc. Let's explore more of the Dark Forces and see how you can use them to create more dangerous dilemmas in your stories.

LAWS OF PHYSICS

Rivers run to the sea, the sun rises and sets, and the stars move across the heavens. Helium balloons escape from toddler's hands, and peanut butter sticks to cat hair. The basic laws of physics confound our desires, sometimes in simple ways, sometimes quite dramatically.

Gravity, magnetism, the motion of the planets and stars follow laws, identified by 17th-century scientist Isaac Newton:

1. Inertia - a body at rest tends to stay at rest; a body in motion tends to stay in motion: snooze alarms, lousy jobs, bad relationships.

2. Force equals mass times acceleration: push harder to go faster, be it car chases, careers, or rockets.

3. For every action there is an opposite and equal reaction: teenagers, reform movements, violence blowback.

A. IN ACTION

When your characters must deal with physical things to achieve their goal — and who doesn't — they're up against the Dark Forces. Gravity can be either amusing or annoying, just ask the baby in the high chair who's dropped a toy ten times, or the babysitter who's picked it up nine. Sunrise is a joy to some but a curse to the vampire who doesn't close the coffin in time.

B. IN MEDIA

Wim Wenders' feature *Fitzcarroldo* and documentary *Burden of Dreams* are about the challenge of building an opera house in the Amazon, including carrying a riverboat over a mountain. The physical challenge of running rapids in *The River Wild* reflected and heightened the personal drama. Martial arts and action-adventure movies use the laws of Nature as barriers to be physically mastered.

TV hero *MacGyver* applied mental skills and used the Dark Forces for good.

Magic seemingly circumvents the laws of physics. Jedi Knights do it. Willow in *Buffy* and the sisters in the *Charmed* series do it. Neo in *The Matrix* does what seems like magic, once he realizes his perception of the laws of physics is an illusion and learns how to use the real laws of that world.

C. IN YOUR CREATIONS

Inner Drives Center of Motivation – Root: the basic physical stuff, & Throat: using intelligence to move stuff around.

Some things stick together; others don't. Any physical problem can be solved with either duct tape or WD-40, right? Similarly, your characters can pull things together (make a raft or a kite to escape) or separate them (remove the fuse from the bomb, cut off the dragon's wings).

Whether it's building a house, climbing a cliff, or baking a cake, characters have to deal with the laws of physics. Of course, if they're wizards or are in other dimensions, some laws might not apply. Change it if you will, but keep it consistent.

We've used force to overcome gravity, and sci-fi stories apply "inertial dampers" to keep ships and people from being shredded at high speeds. Fiction often leads the way where science follows. Explore some laws of physics past the next step and beyond. What's after light speed?

THEORIES OF OTHER PHYSICS

Quantum mechanics, fractals, string theory, indeterminacy...

These concepts entered our consciousness with Einstein, Bose, Heisenberg, and others. They've also entered our stories, but too often with leaps of correspondence that make for fun fantasies, but very little reality.

A. IN ACTION

Hindu philosophy posited many of these theories thousands of years ago and crafted myths to illustrate them (Indra's Net of Gems explains interconnectivity and holograms). Western science is just now catching up. Indeterminacy is mathematically proven but nearly impossible to illustrate. String theory is still controversial. Cosmic rays, radio waves, gamma rays, proton decay, radioactivity — these less obvious aspects of the physical world can seriously harm us (radiation poisoning), as well as help (radiation therapy). The math proposes Dark Matter and Dark Energy make up about 96% of the universe, but to date they've not been found. Alternate universes, worm holes, and time travel have been hallmarks of sci-fi for decades, yet still lie beyond proof and practical use.

B. IN MEDIA

The books *The Dancing Wu Li Masters, The Tao of Physics,* and *Quantum Leadership* move us through observer-determinate dimensions of reality and apply it to our business and personal lives.

The Celestine Prophecies, What the Bleep Do We Know?, and *The Secret* speculate on how to do this with our own minds, as do the many teachings over thousands of years about using the power of attraction to realize your dreams.

Star Trek, Babylon 5, and the classic stories from mid-20th-century sci-fi and fantasy use Dark Force aspects to create challenges and opposition for their characters, shape-shifting, and chasing each other at warp speed through alternate dimensions.

Sliding Doors and *Run, Lola, Run* apply principles of string theory and multiple universes to otherwise ordinary people.

C. IN YOUR CREATIONS

Inner Drives Center of Motivation – Throat: only understanding will solve the dilemmas of these Dark Forces.

Read *Scientific American* and other science journals for story ideas.

Scan world myths for stories that reflect these principles, such as the Hindu myths that seem to refer to nuclear explosions.

Have a scientist or geek in your story explain things for us. Physics on this quantum level is really really tiny, so have your logic well worked out on how it affects our regular world.

Stick to one or two odd-physics devices, such as multiple realities or time travel. More than two is hard for your audience to follow or to believe.

TIME

This Dark Force affects everything in the cosmos and has been personified as Father Time with his reaping scythe, the Greek Fate Atropos whose scissors cut the thread of life, and the Hindu god Shiva whose dance of destruction makes way for new life. The oldest traditions observe vast cycles of time and many cultures built temples to mark these cosmic passages, such as at Borobodur, Angkor Watt, Chichen-Itza, Stonehenge, etc.

Time's Dark Force of entropy and the tendency to balance lead to stasis, which is not only peaceful, but boring and is one good reason to end your dramatic love story or madcap comedy just as the two opposing forces come together in resolution. After that, it's likely to be deadly dull.

The human tendency to savor and cling to our own time is in direct conflict with the fact that time flows. This Dark Force is actually the foundation of all your plotlines and is embodied in the concept of "the ticking clock."

A. IN ACTION

Anti-aging entrepreneurs applaud the steady stream of new customers. Projects have deadlines, trains have timetables, recipes have time-specific directions for whipping or heating. The military has an acronym for it, OBE - Overtaken By Events. Life would simply be impossible if not for the flow of time, yet it puzzles and troubles us so. Good news for you, since audiences will always be interested in a good bout with Time.

B. IN MEDIA

Enter the slow time of Faerie Land and you might not return for twenty years: blink once and your babies are grown; blink twice and your youth is gone.

Peter Pan and the Lost Boys don't want to grow up, and Captain Hook runs from crocodile death, announced by a ticking clock. The entire fable is about holding back the hands of time, or not. Disney's cartoon glosses over the deeper philosophy so poignantly played out in P.J. Hogan's 2003 film.

In Richard Matheson's love story *Somewhere in Time,* Christopher Reeve goes back sixty years to reunite with the younger version of an aging actress who begs him to return. The inciting incident in *The First Wives Club* is husbands putting aside their middle-aged wives for new ones.

Time is a major factor in *Star Trek, Back to the Future, Time Rider, A Winter's Tale, Portrait of Dorian Gray, Brigadoon,* the Omega 13 in *Galaxy Quest,* the disappearance of *Babylon 4,* Jules Verne's *The Time Machine,* Julian May's *Many-Colored Land* novels, *Dune, The Matrix, A Wrinkle in Time, World Enough and Time,* and many more.

C. IN YOUR CREATIONS

Inner Drives Center of Motivation – Ajna: control of time.

An Ajna focus character will have paranormal abilities and an omniscient sense of awareness, like the Kwisatz Haderach of Frank Herbert's *Dune* novels, who can be all places at once and go backwards and forwards in time.

Many fighters say time slows down during combat, like it did for Neo in *The Matrix*. Experiment with different characters operating on different time speeds.

There's an excellent montage of changing time in *Notting Hill* as Hugh Grant's character strolls along a street and seasons change a couple of times during that one walk.

Your time-travel stories should always offer a fresh perspective, a new slant on the story's original problem. Perhaps show how what is "bad" was once "good," or reveal the eventual downside of a seemingly good idea.

The personal desire to slow or stop the passage of time, often through red sports cars or blond hair color, offers universal story opportunities (*Death Becomes Her*).

If your hero's running away from a problem, show the problem's life cycle with at least three of these distinct phases: how it began, what could have solved it then, what failed to work, how it grew, how it will all end, what the results will be. Having gained insights via time travel, or astute observation, your heroine can now apply her acquired wisdom to the problem.

DUALITY

The nature of the universe dictates opposites: up/down, dark/light, cold/hot, male/female, etc. The polarity of the bar magnet produces the magnetic field that allows actual work to be done. Computers run on a binary system. Genetic diversity, in a test tube or a body, requires polarity. Playing up duality in your stories increases dramatic conflict.

A. IN ACTION

Seasonal extremes and night-and-day dualities usually play background roles in stories. Our biological clocks are attuned to these rhythms and often marked by ceremonies as ancient as our awareness. Christmas, Easter, Halloween, and many religious festivals are tied to dualities of summer/winter solstices and fall/spring equinoxes.

Societies often use nature's dualities to justify gender inequality and the disparity between rich and poor. E.g., masculine solar = strong and energetic, feminine lunar = weak and reflective (although in the ancient goddess religions it was just the opposite).

B. IN MEDIA

When Harry Met Sally is an example of the Dark Force of gender duality. Harry's masculine viewpoint resists the possibility of Sally's equality, as well as the challenge of sexual duality ruining their friendship. Sally is suspicious of Harry's masculine motives and skeptical of his ability to resist the dual sexual standards. Their story is about overcoming polarization.

Screwball comedies such as *Adam's Rib* and *Bringing Up Baby* progress from warring opposites to collaborating dualities as both man and woman eventually see and accept the value in what each brings to the party.

The 1980s comedy *Nine to Five* is about working women convincing their misogynist boss-man, through trickery and force, that duality should be a positive thing, not an archaic oppression mechanism.

Daylight, the flip side of night, is a vital element in *Buffy the Vampire Slayer*, Ann Rice's *Vampire Chronicles*, and all vampire tales because sunlight destroys vampires.

Onset of winter is the challenge in some sagas. Award-winning docu-drama *The Journals of Knud Rasmussen* tracks an Inuit tribe's survival tactics. In Mary Shelley's *Frankenstein* the Doctor and his creation flee north to the icy Arctic, away from their temperate home.

Dr. Zhivago, Lawrence of Arabia, and *The English Patient* all juxtapose harsh remote areas with sophisticated urban settings, helping to symbolize the conflict between society's expectations and the characters' own desires.

C. IN YOUR CREATIONS

Inner Drives Center of Motivation - Solar Plexus, both Lower & Aspirational: the home of duality.

Use duality of clothes (princess vs. prostitute), dialogue (stock broker vs. street rapper), or setting (desert vs. oasis) to signal a change in message or conflict.

Illustrate your character's arc by showing his progress from initial resistance to eventual acceptance and working *with* the other thing/person in a duality. *Romancing the Stone* is a great example of this: Kathleen Turner's character goes from girly-girl romance writer to brave adventuress as she arcs from initial conflict with Michael Douglas' rogue character to working together towards a mutual goal.

As simple a thing as heating up coffee or cooling down on a hot day can illustrate this Dark Force — we must expend effort to mold Nature's dualities to our will.

EARTH, AIR, FIRE, AND WATER

All mythologies personify the elements and give them backstories: thunderbirds, ocean gods, fire lizards, airy-fairies, the Fall of Atlantis, the Flood (most cultures have this myth).

Mythologized or not, earthquakes, high winds, wildfires, droughts, floods, and tsunamis are constant reminders that Nature is bigger than us and must always be taken into account.

A. IN ACTION

See more at CNN and The Weather Channel. Watch Al Gore's movie *An Inconvenient Truth.*

Floods and storms yearly plague the same places, yet people still live there, defiant against the Dark Forces, or just plain stupid.

B. IN MEDIA

The world's myths are full of disaster stories just waiting to be updated.

Earth - In *Galaxy Quest* Captain Taggart (Tim Allen) unsuccessfully battles a rock monster that has "no motivation and no vulnerable spots," Technology saves the day. Mountain climbers are going up against the earth. *Lawrence of Arabia* battles and conquers desert sands, as do the Fremen of *Dune.*

Fire - Titan god Prometheus felt sorry for primitive humans and stole fire from the gods for them, so they could grill mastodons and stay up past dark telling stories around a campfire. He was severely punished for this early version of intellectual property piracy.

Fire is predicted to end this round of reality in many myths. Volcanic fire is the plot driver in *Last Days of Pompeii, Krakatoa East of Java,* and *Volcano.* The movie *Backdraft* features firemen. And don't forget *Bambi* and that scary forest fire.

Water - Sea god Neptune thwarts Odysseus' return to Ithaca in *The Odyssey.* Hercules' boyfriend Hylas is seduced by water nymphs and Herc misses the boat, literally, as Jason and the rest of the Argonauts sail on for the Golden Fleece.

Other water stories are *Poseidon Adventure, The Perfect Storm, Waterworld,* and *The Day After.* Novelist Clive Cussler's hero Dirk Pitt is a primo scuba diver, so many adventures take place in and around water. The 2004 Southeastern Asia tsunami and 2005 Hurricane Katrina are already mythologized in story and song.

Air – *Twister* is all about tornadoes. Judi Dench is an air elemental in *The Chronicles of Riddick.* American Indians have a Thunderbird deity and some winds are named. Zephyr is the Greek west wind, a demon boss in the game *Castlevania: Dawn of Sorrow,* and a character in the *Golden Sun* game. Some prophecies about the early 21st century predict killer windstorms, rather like those hitting Europe these days.

Kim Stanley Robinson's *Mars* novels deal with all four elements as humans terraform Mars, and sea levels rise on Earth from climate change.

C. IN YOUR CREATIONS

Inner Drives Center of Motivation – Root: sheer survival.

What makes disaster films interesting is how people react to the disaster: some shine, some slink away, some shatter.

Use the universal symbolism of the elements. Water = emotions. Air = spirituality. Fire = mind. Earth = body. In a scene with two people, put the emotional one in front of the water, so when we look at them we see that emotion symbol. Work the other symbols into action or dialogue to enhance your meaning, such as lovers arguing in the rain.

Take us back in time to experience the shattering of a world or the collapse of a civilization via one of these elements.

Follow the Stealing Fire From Heaven theme and have your Prometheus bring some new element to the situation that counters these Dark Forces (crossbows, electricity, computers) and angers the establishment. Perhaps he escapes Prometheus's punishment, perhaps not.

What if humans could control the weather? Who decides whether it'll rain or not? How could that go bad?

Global warming is already changing things, including sea levels. Explore ways we can head it off, deal with it, or not.

RED IN TOOTH AND CLAW

Nature is not all butterflies and cuddly kittens. It's also brutal, bloody, and downright nasty. But hey, don't take it personally, that's just how it is. You know, *The Lion King* "circle of life" thing.

Many of our problems with animals are territorial. Even today elephants and tigers kill humans if they're forced out of their natural habitats. Predators and creepy-crawlies naturally tweak our fight-or-flight genes. Perhaps it's genetic memories of earlier days when we ran from saber-toothed tigers and literally swam with the sharks. The animal kingdom can provide exciting dangers and obstacles for your characters.

A. IN ACTION

Many mythologies use animals to symbolize characteristics: wise owls, crafty foxes, courageous lions, loyal dogs, lone eagles, etc. In some initiatory systems the aspirant acquires an animal spirit guide. Because we are related to animals and recapitulate that heritage in our gestation process, some imagine we can shape shift into various animals if our will, or our drugs, are strong enough. *Emerald Forest* plays on this theme, as do the *Dune* novels and *Altered States*.

Animal trainers always advise respect for the animals since they're wild first, tame second. Many trainers and zoo workers have paid a high price for forgetting this. Big game hunters have shivery stories of cunning animals who tracked them down years after an encounter and others who even set traps for the humans.

TV's Crocodile Hunter Steve Irwin was killed by a stingray. It was totally impersonal, but it tragically illustrates that old adage: Stay out of Nature's way and She won't kill you.

B. IN MEDIA

Enkidu of Mesopotamian myth and Siegfried of Norse myth both understood the language of animals. *Aesop's Fables* and most fairy tales are full of tricky and treacherous animals.

Mothra, Willard, Snakes on a Plane, the snakes in *Raiders of the Lost Ark, The Edge, The Ghost and the Darkness, Predator, Arachnophobia, A Cry in the Dark* ("Dingo got my baybee!"), the hyenas in *The Lion King,* and of course, *Jaws.*

Though he must leave them for the world of humans, *The Jungle Book*'s Mowgli fully understands the beasts who raised him. So too does the researcher in *Never Cry Wolf.* Werewolf stories give lycopanthic characteristics to humans; a classic is *An American Werewolf in London.* In the book and movie *Altered States,* a scientist genetically reverts to an earlier animal, as also happened in a *Star Trek: The Next Generation* episode where the Klingon Warf became a wolf, someone reverted to a lizard, and... did Data turn into an abacus or a pocket calculator?

Extreme animals make for spooky movies: *Them, The Birds, The Thing, Cujo, Tremors, Jurassic Park,* and the behemoth sandworms of *Dune.* How about those pigs (cops) in the chilling socio-political satire *Animal Farm?*

And then there's the archetypal *Moby Dick,* that great white whale who seems to have a personal vendetta against Captain Ahab, who certainly has one against him for taking off his leg. It's a perfect storm of Dweller on the Threshold versus a Dark Force.

C. IN YOUR CREATIONS

Inner Drives Center of Motivation – Root: survival.

We tend to humanize animal behavior, often to disastrous ends. A psychologically perceptive story such as *Moby Dick* will show why we do that, and why it's not a good idea.

The terror of animals out of control is buried deep in our genes and can supply endless amounts of drama — use it well, and you can create truly horrifying Dark Force tales.

When hunter-conservationist Jim Corbett tracked man-eating tigers in India, he'd wear a mask on the back of his head because tigers usually attack from behind. Have your character learn animal ways and use that against them.

Heroines who can commune with animals offer unique story paths. Explore this favorite tool of children's stories in a different direction: instead of animals teaching humans, go vise-versa. Or have animals incensed at how humans are ruining their planet and deciding to wipe us out.

Update the stories of human/animal mixes such as centaurs. In the TV series *Dark Angel,* the genetically engineered heroine Max has cat genes and qualities.

Explore the shape-shifting concept. If you could flip gene switches for instant expression of other qualities, what could your characters become and do? Fly? Burrow? Run like a cheetah?

A PLAGUE ON BOTH YOUR HOUSES

Epidemics, pandemics, plagues, etc. are impersonal Dark Forces, though they can be wielded by humans to ill ends. Viruses and bacteria are tiny. Plagues are huge and horrifying. It's normal for one person to be sick. It's just wrong wrong wrong when thousands or even millions fall ill and die.

Some say humans are a virus infecting planet earth and that plagues are nature's way of running a fever and combating the disease that is us. Others say humans are simply breeding grounds and mobile hosts for bacteria and viruses who really rule the world.

A. IN ACTION

The Black Death plagued Asia, Europe, and the Middle East for many centuries, wiping out millions. Diseases introduced by colonizing Europeans destroyed a significant part of the populace in the Americas and the Pacific. The Spanish Flu pandemic just after World War I killed 50-100 million people while only ten million died in the War.

World travelers are advised to get vaccinated against diseases we had thought under control: smallpox, yellow fever, cholera, typhoid, polio, etc. Plus, we're still fighting dengue fever, sleeping sickness, malaria, river blindness, tick fever, etc.

Legionnaire's Disease, anthrax scares, mad cow disease, bird flu, AIDS... causes often spring from something fixable such as pest control, common hygiene, common sense, preventive medicine. Global warming allows more pests to thrive, upping incidences of disease.

Antibiotics have unintentionally created immune strains of some diseases, undermining our defense mechanisms. The fad for exotic pets increases risk of zoonotic (animal-to-human) diseases such as bird flu, Ebola from monkeys, SARS from cats, and new ailments from hamsters, iguanas, and other "pocket pets."

B. IN MEDIA

Humans demand meaning and often attribute diseases to angry gods, evil conspiracies, or the wickedness of the victims. The Old

Testament story of Moses features plagues of frogs, lice, flies, locusts, etc. as Yahweh's tools of persuading Pharaoh to let his people go.

The Decameron is a series of racy stories written as diversion from the 14th-century Bubonic plague. Plague is a plot driver in *Dangerous Beauty*, as a courtesan is accused by the Catholic Church of bringing God's wrath down on Venice. Ingmar Bergman's *The Seventh Seal* is set against plague, and Death is a character.

Read Stephen King's *The Stand* and you'll freak out at a sneeze. Tom Clancy's *Executive Order* presaged current bio-war events. The films *Outbreak, The Andromeda Strain,* and *Twelve Monkeys* all deal with this deadly Dark Force. *Philadelphia, Longtime Companion,* and *Angels in America* explore social and personal issues around AIDS.

Germ warfare has been around since Caesar's cook secretly added herbs to the enemy's beer to cause diarrhea. An entire season of Fox TV's *24* dealt with a deadly plague and the Counter Terrorism Unit's efforts to contain it.

C. IN YOUR CREATIONS

Inner Drives Center of Motivation – Root: survival, & Throat: using smarts to survive.

The impersonality of epidemics makes them terrifying: You can't reason with them, call a truce, or buy them off. But oh, how fascinating it is to watch people try to do so. Show us the many ways people are affected by epidemics: who panics, who's calm, who runs, who stays to help, who uses it to their advantage, who thinks so far out of the Petri dish they save the day... or not.

The scramble for explanations offers rich possibilities: who blames gods, who blames victims, who refuses to blame and sets about solving the problem?

Show the consequences of thoughtlessness or stupidity: feeding cow bits to cows = mad cow disease; draining sewage into drinking water = cholera; dirty air filters = Legionnaire's Disease, etc.

The consequences of politics and bureaucracy can also be tragic: funds pledged to fight AIDS are held up by religious ideology or political power plays; funds intended for charity end up with terrorists.

Explore the psychology of germ warfare perpetrators: why this scattershot approach claiming innocents, instead of pinpoint accuracy targeting your enemy?

As biological warfare and pandemics lodge more deeply in our common psyche, we'll need more stories about this. The more science and common sense you can add the better because neither punishment nor prayer has ever worked well against this impersonal, insidious Dark Force.

Techno troubles

Robots gone wild, pollution, depleted uranium... sometimes technology is not our friend. Creators often have problems with their creations. The Judeo-Christian Yahweh faced rebellion both with angels in heaven and humans down in the Garden of Eden. Problems with his faulty humans continued such that floods, exiles, plagues, wars, and enslavement seemed necessary to get them back in line. None of it ever worked very well, though. Still doesn't.

Hindu scriptures say we have problems with this universe because it's made up of the faulty stuff left over from the last *manvantara* (universe), where Matter held sway over Spirit. Christianity personalizes this as individual Original Sin, for which we must accept, earn, or buy redemption, depending on the sect.

Human creators also encounter problems with their products, especially if they've done faulty Quality Control. Gepetto carved Pinocchio and the ungrateful boy ran off with thugs. Dr. Frankenstein, grief-stricken by his mother's death, animated a patchy corpse, who ungratefully demanded a girlfriend and caused mayhem when his will was thwarted.

In strategic military planning this "oops" concept is called 3rd, 4th, and 5th level consequences. In common language, it's called Murphy's Law. Or to quote Rosanna Dana Dana from the early days of *Saturday Night Live*, "It's always something."

A. IN ACTION

We all have ideas on how to better the world, hence the popularity of world-building games such as *Age of Mythology, The Sims,* and *Spore.* Myths, fiction, sci-fi, and fantasy feed this hunger to be creative, even if secondhand.

Technology is usually leaps and bounds ahead of the science that discovered it, much less the psychology of the users. University and government Ethics Departments attempt to address these issues, but technology moves at the speed of thought, and rational thinking about technology moves at glacial speed.

B. IN MEDIA

Since the dish ran away with the spoon and puppet Pinocchio wanted to become a real boy, we've told stories about our technology turning against us. Astrology explains some mechanical hiccups as Mercury in retrograde; so, weld a fin to that errant planet and your hard drive will never crash?

Pygmalion & Galatea, Svengali & Trilby, Pinocchio, "Petrushka," "Capellia," and *Frankenstein* are classic stories, ballets, and operas on the concept of a smart guy molding a statue, a girl, bits of wood, or body parts into something different and supposedly better.

Some movies and musicals are *My Fair Lady, Vertigo, Gypsy, Educating Rita, Mona Lisa, Mannequin, The Perfect Man, Pretty*

Woman, The Little Mermaid, Blade Runner, Short Circuit, Honey I Shrunk the Kids, Lawnmower Man, Data on *Star Trek, Millennium Man, A.I., I, Robot,* and all Frankenstein films.

No-tech, low-tech, or bad-tech stories play on our fascination with and fear of our creations: *Road Warrior, Westworld, War Games, The Terminator, Tank Girl,* and the TV series *Dark Angel.* And don't forget that smooth-talking, creepy supercomputer HAL from *2001: A Space Odyssey.*

The demise of computers is a plot driver and character molder in many sci-fi stories, including the *Dune* novels, where super-smart human Mentats take over the jobs of computers. Manmade clones and droids battle it out pretty mindlessly in *Star Wars* movies, as do the Uruk Hai in *The Lord of the Rings.* But the Cylons in *Battlestar Galactica* pose sophisticated philosophical dilemmas, having self-evolved beyond mere machines to become idealistic, feeling humanoids.

C. IN YOUR CREATIONS

Inner Drives Center of Motivation - Throat: conscious creativity, science, literature, media.

The creator can be driven by love of logic, science, and technology, a desire to see what can be done. They're often unconcerned about consequences because they've got the antidote, are distanced by space ("GM foods aren't grown in my area"), or time ("I'll be dead by then").

As others warn of consequences, your Pygmalion rationalizes that if it's all One Life, and if Separatism is the great sin, then genetic engineering mixing human and rice genes, chicken and tomato genes, etc. could be a step towards total unification. Or, have them quite willing to pay personal consequences for a supposedly greater good.

Technology, like electricity, or the Force of *Star Wars*, is neither good nor bad; show us this impersonal aspect both before and alongside of how it's being ill-used by your characters.

There can be no redemption without realization, whether by the creator or the creature. Dramatic tension enters when they don't agree on the nature of redemption (*Frankenstein*) and/or move at different speeds (*Battlestar Galactica*).

CONCLUSION

The impersonal Dark Forces of the world around us offer myriad opportunities for obstacles, challenges, and occasional allies for your stories. Add to those listed here. Expand a single incident into a snowballing major dilemma. Peer around the edges of normality for a unique perspective to open our minds to new realities.

With at least one Dark Force problem in your story, ideally one that reflects or enhances your theme or characters, you offer a richer relationship with your people and plot. Remember, the Force is always with you, and it's up to you and your characters whether it's Dark or not... and Dark is usually much more interesting.

4.
THE DARK BROTHERHOOD
— SUPRA-PERSONAL

+ **Who is this Dark Brotherhood?**

+ **Where did they come from?**

+ **What do they want?**

+ **How do they get away with it?**

+ **How can we resist and/or defeat them?**

You've transformed all your Dwellers on the Threshold and overcome inertia, procrastination, etc., but still can't get that earth-changing project off the page and onto the screen? Is it the Dark Brotherhood holding you back? Ummm, probably not, unless you're a really bright Light who can affect the lives of millions and change the course of history. Of course, we storytellers do have that ambition, and modern media now does have that reach, so maybe...

Are there really uber-powerful entities out to control the cosmos? Do deities play dice with lives and marbles with galaxies? And do the bad ones cheat?

Who knows? It's impossible to prove one way or the other in real life, but for the sake of story, let's explore. Some of this is already covered in the "What Dark Side?" chapter; here we're specifically talking about powerful supra-personal entities, rather than just Evil as a concept or force.

WHO IS THIS DARK BROTHERHOOD?

Often called the Dark Brotherhood, DB, or Black Magicians, this category also includes women, aliens, gods, demons, and nonhuman creatures. In many traditions these are former or current creators or rulers of the worlds they still strive to control. *The Morning of the Magicians* book is full of world legends about lost civilizations, Black Magicians, and manipulation of worlds.

Does the DB exist? Certainly there are always a select few beings at the top who run things, and not everyone agrees with them. Scurrilous or scapegoats, this pattern is a constant in human affairs. Are they as evil as the *Star Wars* films' Evil Emperor and Darth Vader? Do they generate genocide? Or are all our evils homegrown? Most mythologies attribute atrocious things to the DB, whether out of reluctance to believe humans can be so horrid as to originate the awful things we do to each other, or reluctance to ascribe such wretchedness as befalls us to our otherwise benevolent gods.

A line in Malcolm Lowry's *Under the Volcano* suggests that if humans sobered up for three days, we'd die of shame on the fourth. Maybe this Dark Brotherhood idea is just a way to shunt aside our burden of guilt. Then again, maybe not.

WHERE DO THEY COME FROM?

Often from other worlds, eons, or dimensions. Lucifer and the Fallen Angels came from heaven. In *Babylon 5,* the dark Shadows are an ancient race back for one last try at conquering civilized space. Sumerian myths tell of extra-planetary resource hunters; *Stargate* expands on that idea. In *Buffy the Vampire Slayer,* the high school sits over a hell mouth through which a really big bad guy tries to enter our reality.

Atlanteans, Lemurians, Mayans, the Thule, and the Anasazi are often said to have fallen because of DB influences, usually via a misuse of magic skills.

Like *Star Wars'* Jedi Knights gone Sith, both Black and White Magicians train in the same system, up to a certain point. One reason the Wisdom training is so difficult is to hopefully weed out the bad and the weak. Remember all those warnings the Jedi Masters scowled about young Anakin Skywalker, and how he just didn't fit in with the program early on? If only they'd listened to themselves.

On the other hand, all-powerful gods who dispense good and evil bear a striking resemblance to grown-ups when we ourselves are young, small, and powerless. The hold-over desire to have somebody big fix things, and the tendency to placate their moods to avoid punishment, can lead to cowering worship to guarantee good harvests. Spinning off of this tendency, conspiracy theories and religions offer the comforting idea that even in the midst of chaos and suffering, there's *somebody* in control.

WHAT DO THEY WANT?

Power. More power. All the power. But just for them. Power is a deadly addictive drug that can make you very selfish. In the progress towards enlightenment, the DB stops at the point that requires self sacrifice, so you can bet that anything they do is to their advantage, even if it looks otherwise.

HOW DO THEY GET AWAY WITH IT?

Balloon payments, like *The Portrait of Dorian Gray* where a young man's portrait ages and shows his sins, while he stays beautiful... until the end. The Black Magician can divert Karma and consequences onto her followers, often by convincing them the suffering is good for their souls. Or, she can magically hold it at bay for lots of lifetimes, but then suffer horridly when it all comes due. Like lots of real estate speculations, it seems like a good deal at the time. In *Harry Potter,* Voldemort did a "flight from death" to postpone his Karma and bespelled Morfin to falsely confess to the murders of Voldemort's father and grandparents.

The Dark Magician aligns with other DBs, can be strengthened by the devotion of humans, and is a master of illusion. They get humans to be the front men, like the politicians and power brokers in *X-Files* who worked for the aliens. And then there were the Nazis, Fascists of all stripes, the Janjaweed of 21st-century Darfur, and otherwise ordinary humans swept up in mob genocide. We often pay so much attention to the perpetrators that we ignore the instigators who might or might not be the Dark Brotherhood.

Disbelief. If no one believes you exist, you can get away with all sorts of evil because people will just pretend they don't see it. In *The Hitchhiker's Guide to the Galaxy* Douglas Adams calls this an SEP: Somebody Else's Problem.

HOW CAN WE RESIST AND/OR DEFEAT THEM?

Ignorance and apathy are effective DB tools. If we don't know and/or don't care, they can get away with almost anything. If all it takes for Evil to triumph is the indifference of good people, move from passive to active and challenge them.

Higher frequencies can sometimes protect you from lower Dark frequencies, so always try to take the high road. See more in "Confronting the Dark Side." Thankfully, the DB is ultimately like everything else: It carries within it the seeds of its own destruction... if you can afford to wait that long.

CONCLUSION

'Tis all a Chequer-board of Nights and Days
Where Destiny with Men for Pieces plays:
Hither and thither moves, and mates, and slays,
And one by one back in the Closet lays.
"The Rubaiyat of Omar Khayyam" translated by Edward
Fitzgerald

Who knows, maybe the Atlantean (lunar) and Aryan (solar) sorcerers did duke it out in the battle between Good and Evil eons ago. Maybe Greek gods Athena and Poseidon really did influence Odysseus' ten-year journey home from the Trojan War. Perhaps the Illuminati really does run today's Tri-Lateral Commission, the Prieure de Sion guards the bloodline of Jesus and Mary Magdalene, and the Venusians have lifted the post-Atlantean quarantine around our planet, opening us up again to extraterrestrial visitations. Great stories come from great imaginings and those about the Dark Brotherhood are some of the most imaginative of all.

They Walk on the Dark Side

We've differentiated between aspects of opposition: the Dweller on the Threshold (personal), the Dark Forces (impersonal), and the Dark Brotherhood (supra-personal). Now let's explore archetypes of individuals — human and nonhuman.

Sometimes characters are not complex enough; they're two-dimensional, stereotypical. Sometimes they're too complicated (especially in scripts and plays as opposed to novels), and need to be pared down for clarity. Read over the categories in this section and see which best fits your character's strongest Inner Drive: power, acceptance, survival, accomplishment, etc. The descriptions, examples, and suggestions will help you align with these powerful universal archetypes. Then apply your own personal spin to make unique yet fully believable characters.

Just as the best stories have a plot and one or more subplots, so too will you want to have a main archetype for each character, and then modify it with at least one secondary archetype they are either letting go of or trying to become. Think of Angel and Spike in Buffy the Vampire Slayer — vampires yes, but seriously troubled by curses, computer chips in their brains, or desires to be something else. Captain Jack Sparrow in Pirates of the Caribbean struggles between basic pirate archetype and becoming an antihero, with a bit of the rake tossed in for good measure.

Other sections in this book will help you refine your characters' approaches, actions, oppositions, and allies throughout the story. For now, focus on the category that best suits your character, and also determine a secondary one for deepening their personalities and problems. ∽

5.
THE ANTIHERO

Sometimes it's glaringly obvious who's the bad guy. Other times, not so much. Evil is said to disguise itself as truth and beauty; death and destruction as power and seduction. The Antichrist is a scary idea because we can't always tell the difference between good and evil.

In some traditions Lucifer and the other angels were to serve God, then God created humans and demanded angels serve mankind. This demotion rankled, and Lucifer refused to turn from his first love to serve the puny usurpers. Harsh words flew and war in heaven ensued.

Some hold that Lucifer (which means "light bringer") is the good guy bringing humanity knowledge and freedom via higher consciousness, while Yahweh and his angels suppress us with ignorance and fear via organized religion. *His Dark Materials* trilogy follows this idea.

This paradigm plays out in the antihero, the individual who stands apart from society and breaks its rules. Yet, while sneering at the hypocrisy and corruption of the norm, they uphold a higher ideal and are harbingers of the future.

CHARACTERISTICS

A cynic is just a wounded romantic. Maybe, but they bury it deep within.

Disillusioned. Disgusted. Misanthropic. Self-centered. Often sharp-witted and sharp-tongued. No small talk. Foul language; or, no cursing whatsoever. Physical courage. Analytical mind. Seldom swayed by emotion, they can usually be bought, proving to themselves once again that all humans, even them, are venal.

Because they really don't give a sh*t, they can do the dirty work nobody else will or can do. In Walter Hill's slick rock-and-roll fable *Streets of Fire*, Tom Cody (note the cowboy name) gives the quintessential antihero line when he shrugs and remarks that guys like him always get sent to do the tough jobs.

Though very self-centered, when a greater good serves their own purposes, they go along, like Adam Baldwin's character Jayne in Joss Whedon's *Serenity* and *Firefly*.

A. IN ACTION

Antiheroes typically arise from over-regulated, corrupt, declining societies. They uphold the true ideal which the rest of society now just mocks or ignores.

Cultures follow a cycle from the founding in hardship, idealism, and innovation; the settling-in-and-civilizing; the growing sophistication; the over-regulation and over-indulgence; the decline and fall.

Because they harken back to the good old days, rough-and-ready antiheroes are more popular in a culture's stories when people are disillusioned in the over-regulation stage and beyond. During the settling-in-and-civilizing and the sophistication stages, there is little sign of the antihero, as people deny their uncouth roots. Odysseus of *Iliad* fame, for instance, went from positive "wise" to negative "wily" over a couple hundred years in ancient Greece as the populace became more citified.

Gilgamesh of the Middle East, England's Robin Hood, and depending on whether you were French or English, Joan of Arc, are real-life antiheroes.

Reilly, Ace of Spies, starring Sam Neill, is a suspenseful, sensual miniseries about an actual British superspy torn between his own dark desires and expedient loyalties in the early 1900s.

Al Swearingen in the HBO series *Deadwood* is based on a real person. He's venal, vile, and violent but also inspires fierce loyalty and utter confidence. At rare moments, his almost tender compassion for a few select others is revealed. His actions are for both his own good and the good of the growing frontier community of *Deadwood,* for which he's perfectly willing to slit your throat.

B. IN MEDIA

Antiheroes can be cast out or be outcasts by choice, as in the films *Rebel Without a Cause, Taxi Driver, Chinatown, One Flew Over the Cuckoo's Nest, Midnight Cowboy, Dirty Harry,* and *Payback,* where Mel Gibson is a bad guy with a serious case of revenge for bigger bad guys.

The Japanese story of the 47 Ronin, Samurai without a master but still driven by honor to avenge him, has been told many times in Japanese films. Robert De Niro stars in the action-thriller *Ronin,* playing a modern C.I.A. version of this antihero. *Rambo* leans close to that archetype.

The Bride (Uma Thurman) in Quentin Tarantino's *Kill Bill* films is an effective antiheroine, whose slowly revealed history makes us more and more compassionate for this killing machine. Her strong sense of justice even compels her to kill people she loves — or used to love, until they done her wrong.

Vin Diesel in the *Chronicles of Riddick* is a really bad man out to fight a really evil empire and save the universe. The *Boondock Saints* are brothers who assassinate mob figures in Boston because so-called good men are indifferent and the courts are ineffectual.

Antiheroes often arise in apocalyptic, sci-fi, and action-adventure settings: *Mad Max, Road Warrior, Thunderdome, Waterworld,* and *The Fifth*

Element. One of the best is the swashbuckling yet sensitive Captain Jack Sparrow (Johnny Depp) in *The Pirates of the Caribbean* movies.

On the less lethal side, since they're mostly just skewering convention, are TV characters Larry Sanders, Archie Bunker, Dr. Gregory House, Bart Simpson, and the little monsters in *South Park*.

C. IN YOUR CREATIONS

Inner Drives Center of Motivation - Aspirational Solar Plexus masquerading as Lower Solar Plexus.

Be sure the society in which your antihero operates is moving towards or entrenched in over-regulation, decline, or decay.

Use a tenet of the culture currently ignored by most people as the watchword of the antiheroine: freedom, liberty, equality, justice, peace, prosperity, etc. She brings back the true meaning of the ideal, often by showing how horridly corrupted it is.

How much Darkness is a little, how much is too much? Show ways of balancing the bad things that have to be done with the good of what President Lincoln called "the better angels of our nature."

Antiheroes in the old film noir genre, such as John Garfield, Robert Stack, and Robert Mitchum, had great dialogue establishing their roles, rather than just physical violence. In your stories, show us the psychological context; why are these people renegades? Don't just cut to the action; show us what they're fighting for or against; give us understandable reasons.

Rogue Warriors are great antiheroes. Have an honorable backstory, a time they fought valiantly for the Good, the True, the Beautiful, but then were disillusioned or disinherited. At heart, they still long to serve the higher cause.

In *Measure for Measure*, Shakespeare observed, "They say the best men are molded out of faults, and, for the most, become much more the better for being a little bad."

6.
BAD BOYS AND GIRLS

+ The Trickster

+ The Rake and the Temptress

+ Pimps, Panderers, and Pushers

+ Mommie Dearest and Bad Dads

+ Killer Kids

+ Evil Twins

+ Pirates, Rebels, and Traitors

+ Bad Cop, Worse Cop

+ Bumblers

+ Dictators, Tyrants, and Cult Leaders

+ Mad Scientists

+ Psychopaths, Pedophiles, and Serial Killers

What is it about bad boys and bitches that is so darn attractive?

They personify our own internal rebel, the one we aren't coura-geous enough to be. They challenge our mores and beliefs about proper behavior. They give us a chance to be saviors. They also challenge our own powers of seduction. Some primitive part of us still loves the chase, and like a cheetah cub, we don't recognize food unless it's running away from us. The unobtainable, scary, dangerous person is exciting.

Some of us become bad boys and bitches around weak-willed or needy people. Something about cringing just brings out the bully. Animal instinct to cull the herd or spiritual instinct to heal the world? Not a pretty picture either way, but a very interesting one.

Sometimes it's a supreme selfishness, most often found in creative types. They're married to the Muse, their creativity takes first place, and frankly, if you can't handle it, too bad for you, but it's not their problem.

Here are some archetypes of Bad Boys and Bitches. If your character fits any of these, there is a wealth of examples from life, psychology, and media to inspire the development of traits and foibles. Then add your own unique spin and voila — an exciting new character.

THE TRICKSTER

Most mythologies include a trickster god who's always getting the better of pompous or silly people. The medieval court jester injected perspective and self deprecation to keep the regent mindful that it's all just a game. Some tricksters are malevolent, like the jealous Norse god Loki, responsible for the death of the beloved god Baltar. Southwest American Indians find their god Coyote sharp, but not so deadly.

CHARACTERISTICS

Mentally sharp. Sharp tongue. Good command of language, twists words and phrases, double entendres, puns. Somewhat mean, sometimes downright cruel.

A. IN ACTION

Royal courts traditionally had a jester to break tensions, deflate egos, and entertain. Modern court jesters are media comedians, political cartoonists, satirists. Their sharp tongues and pens puncture the pomposity of assumed power and cry shrilly that not only is the emperor quite naked, he's ill-formed as well. The establishment loathes the Trickster; the populace usually loves him.

B. IN MEDIA

This is not the comic relief in a story. The Trickster is strong and calculating, not a buffoon — though he may play one on TV. Think *Batman*'s Joker.

The Daily Show's Jon Stewart and Stephen Colbert, *Saturday Night Live*, Gary Trudeau's *Doonesbury*, *The Simpsons,* and *South Park* all skewer convention and pomposity.

C. IN YOUR CREATIONS

Inner Drives Center of Motivation – Throat: assessing situations, finding weak spots, pointing them out, and/or using them to bring down a power figure or deflate a situation.

Have your Trickster be clever and observant, ask probing questions, and be very facile with language. Using others' faults against them is a favorite maneuver.

Entrapment: have your Trickster ferret out people's secret desires and lure them in for the kill.

Have others underestimate your Trickster and either reveal things they should not or otherwise let their guard down.

Show that softening or redemption ruins this character, as their entire being is about their role to poke and prod.

THE RAKE AND THE TEMPTRESS

Sex can be a doorway to heaven, flinging wide the prison of the self for a joyride through the starry cosmos. It's also a doorway for lots of other stuff, some of it really icky, like manipulation by Rakes and Temptresses.

Our innate desire for union lowers our physical, emotional, and psychic barriers. These people use that lowering of defenses to conquer others for the sheer pleasure of the chase or for darker motives.

Sometimes people are stereotyped into this category simply because of how they look, like cartoon femme fatale Jessica Rabbit in *Who Framed Roger Rabbit?*, who breathily protested she was only drawn bad. Then again, once you know how people perceive you and you keep projecting that appearance....

CHARACTERISTICS

Pheromones gone wild. They exude an aura of irresistibility and they know it. Some don't actually enjoy sex, but they use sex to gain power and control. Some may be searching for sexual fulfillment, coldly angry they've never found it. They're not always physically beautiful, but they instinctively know what *you* think is beautiful and play that up. They quickly assess your pride (hair, profession, etc.) and your shame (weight, family, etc.) and use those to seemingly bond with you. They can boff you for days and murmur all the love words, but there's always a deep chasm and a steep wall between you and their real self.

A. IN ACTION

The aging Roman Emperor Claudius was felled in part by his seductive, teenage vixen wife, whose insatiable sexual and political appetites extended to most of the Roman Senate.

Texas law used to look the other way if a man shot his wife and her lover. After all, like the jailbird babes sing in *Chicago*, they had it comin'.

The honey trap is a standard ploy in a spy's toolbox, and there are rumors of special espionage sex schools.

B. IN MEDIA

Jewish lore says Adam's first wife was headstrong Lilith. She was too sexually demanding (wanted to be on top), so he put her aside and got the supposedly more submissive Eve. That worked out real well, didn't it? And remember Frazier Crane's demon wife Lilith from *Cheers* and *Frasier*.

Casanova, Mozart's opera "Don Giovanni," *The Portrait of Dorian Gray, I Claudius, Dangerous Liaisons, The Wedding Crashers, Looking for Mister Goodbar, Fatal Attraction, Basic Instinct, The Last Seduction, Bound, Secretary, Chicago.*

Film noir classic *Double Indemnity* shows with shadows, long looks, and an ankle bracelet how femme fatale Barbara Stanwyck lures gullible Fred MacMurray into murdering her husband for the insurance, then betrays him in the end. *Body Heat* tells a similar steamy story, much more graphically, with William Hurt and Kathleen Turner.

C. IN YOUR CREATIONS

Inner Drives Center of Motivation – Lower Solar Plexus: narcissistic control over others via sex, & Sacral: sex, sex, and more sex.

The Wisdom Teachings warn that when you have sex with someone you download their Karma. Show how a character starts taking on the qualities, actions, and dialogue of the seducer.

Have a character get into Tantric sex practices and learn how they affect different energies and aspects of self and partner. He could discover these powers with horror, realizing he's been manipulated; or with glee, realizing he can manipulate others.

Slowly reveal this archetype's revulsion for others through cruel words, reluctance for nonsexual contact, or fastidiousness (showering immediately after sex, changing bed sheets, etc.).

Construct a turning point where this ultimate sex machine is knocked over by a simple touch or one tender kiss that begins to crumble her emotional fortress.

Turn the tables. Have your wronged character search out his seducer's deepest (nonsexual) fear or desire and use that as the weapon of revenge.

PIMPS, PANDERERS, AND PUSHERS

These are really bad guys because they slave out other humans to the lowest desires of still other humans. Not to say that sex and lust aren't simply basic desires, but when you're enslaving a person to your own economic advantage, well, that's like, um, slavery.

Getting innocent people hooked on addictive substances is simply evil. Offering someone a martini? Yeah, the dividing line here is vague, isn't it? Is evil a factor of whether or not it's illegal? Legal substances like tobacco and alcohol cause plenty of harm, yet unlike during Prohibition, those who make and sell them aren't incarcerated.

CHARACTERISTICS

Control freaks. Users. People intent on wallowing in the degradation of others. Low self regard and low regard of others. Pessimistic. Defeatist. Cynical. Greedy. Sociopaths.

A. IN ACTION

Read history. Watch the news. Drive past a drug-sales street corner. Cruise the red-light district. Go to a nightclub. Go to a courthouse and observe pusher/dealer/user trials.

B. IN MEDIA

Scarface was so over the top it became a comedy. *Traffic* is a troubling, personal look at drug dealing. *City of God* illustrates both the lure and the dangers of pushing drugs, via two friends growing up in the slums of Rio de Janeiro.

Anne Bissell's book *Memoirs of a Sex Industry Survivor* gives relevant insights into how girls get involved, and how they get out. *Butterfly 8* with Elizabeth Taylor and *Klute* with Jane Fonda are classic films about call girls caught up in this pattern.

In the HBO series *Deadwood* both Al Swearingen and Cy Tolliver run whores. Their deepest motivations are reflected in their styles of management. Al is crude yet protective. Cy is slick but deadly.

C. IN YOUR CREATIONS

Inner Drives Center of Motivation – Sacral: sex-money-fear, & Lower Solar Plexus: personal power.

Not to make us sympathize but to make us understand, show us how and why a character started dealing or pimping.

Delve into their deeper motivations of displaced love, anger, vengeance, disappointment.

Show why wandering souls are drawn to the discipline and seeming protection of these strong-arm types.

Show how people with low self esteem would be drawn to a profession offering faint praise for who and what you are.

What does it take to walk away? To stay away?

Is this a societal necessity, like toilets and trash collecting? If so, defend that position. If not, how do we evolve out of this continuing tendency?

MOMMIE DEAREST AND BAD DADS

If it weren't for the bonding drug oxytocin, fatigued and frustrated new moms might toss out that messy, squalling little blob of a newborn. Some parents seems a bit short on oxytocin and do just that; postpartum depression is a very real chemical imbalance, with sometimes tragic results.

When a new tomcat comes into a territory, he kills all the kittens and starts new batches to ensure gene-pool purity; are there evolutionary echoes in stepparents and the high percentage of them committing child abuse? There's a reason "red-headed stepchild" has come to mean "poor little thing."

CHARACTERISTICS

Some are incompetent and uncaring. Others are just downright mean. All are selfish. Some are hypocritically nice to the kids in public. Others snub them. Fear and resentment seem the foundation of their attitudes towards the young. Granted some kids do try your patience, and most parents occasionally want to strangle their teenagers, but for most it's a fleeting expression of frustrated parental love.

A. IN ACTION

Child abuse is a huge problem in many parts of the world. Sometimes it's exacerbated by poverty or fundamentalist cultures; sometimes it's just twisted individuals taking out their frustrations on weaker creatures.

One abusive father claimed he "made the kid," so she was his to do with as he wished.

In Munchausen's Syndrome by Proxy, parents cause illness or injury in their children in order to get attention for themselves.

Second (and third and fourth) wives are stereotypically greedy of the family fortune and push aside others' kids; see more in the supermarket tabloids.

B. IN MEDIA

Most mythic heroes are missing at least one parent, and some get stuck with a dysfunctional stepparent. Hercules got the jealous Hera who sent two snakes to strangle him in his cradle, Cinderella's mean stepmom and stepsisters used her as a drudge, and poor Hamlet got his murderous uncle.

Celebrities, notoriously self-centered to begin with, are models for *Mommie Dearest* (Joan Crawford and her coat hangers: cruel) and *Postcards from the Edge* (Carrie Fisher's mom Debbie Reynolds: comedic).

Blue Sky and *The Great Santini* show how the restrictions of military life affect some parents; Jessica Lange is a sensual and psychologically unbalanced Army wife in the former and Robert Duvall is an abusive Marine dad in the latter. Deadly parents feature in the suspense-horror film *Stepfather*, starring Terry O'Quinn, Jack Nicholson's psychotic romp in *The Shining*, the mom in *The Manchurian Candidate*, and in *Beyond Honor* about female genital mutilation.

C. IN YOUR CREATIONS

Inner Drives Center of Motivation - Lower Solar Plexus: power and self-indulgence.

Reveal the damaged personal boundaries of the parent, her wounded sense of self, as in *Divine Secrets of the Ya-Ya Sisterhood*.

Show the adult powerless in one arena (at work, with the spouse) and then wielding power over children to compensate.

Going up against a grown-up can be terrifying for a young child. Explore ways they can get allies or learn coping skills.

Check out the Adult Children of Alcoholics organization for insights into this family dynamic, where kids have to be more mature than the grown-ups.

Abuse breeds abuse, some say. Show two kids going down different paths, one of them breaking out of the cycle of bad parenting.

KILLER KIDS

Some kids just seem to have been born mean, like Lucy Van Pelt in the *Peanuts* cartoons, always yanking the football away from Charlie Brown. Others turn to it for survival, like kids in ghettos and gangs. Gangs of kids beat up outsiders, bully the weak, and act out animal instincts to cull the herd.

CHARACTERISTICS

Selfish. Verbally abusive. Arrogant. Instinctive cruelty — either no real grasp of others' pain and the finality of death, or a too-real grasp of it and a fascination with it.

Or the quiet, shy type who ultimately takes to the tower with a rifle.

A. IN ACTION

Bullies have always been around, pulling wings off flies and sticking gullible kid's tongues to icy things. Nowadays the bullies, or their victims, are often armed and really dangerous. School shootings, often a backlash to bullying, are all too common.

Some blame violent computer games, some blame lack of parental supervision, others the schools, still others the hormones in food, etc. Wise observers see the entire system as faulty and address it with programs involving entire communities.

Child soldiers are forced into violence; if their empathy circuits get fried, redemption is unlikely. Some kids simply never wire up those circuits; they're the psychopaths.

B. IN MEDIA

The young killers in *The Bad Seed* and *Village of the Damned* were horrifying in the mid 1900s, back when most kids seemed innocent and post WWII life seemed safe. Then came *Rosemary's Baby, The Omen,* and their spawn.

Originally a Japanese film, the 2002 American remake of *The Ring* is a horrifying excursion into the twisted psyche of a troubled child.

Draco Malfoy comes close to killing in the *Harry Potter* series. Youngsters in *His Dark Materials* get into killing spots, with various psychologically complex reactions and actions.

Acclaimed film *City of God* follows the lives of two boys growing up in the favelas (slums) of Rio and how the act of killing affects them differently.

C. IN YOUR CREATIONS

Inner Drives Center of Motivation – Root: killer instinct, & Lower Solar Plexus: selfish power mongering.

Show early fascination with the way bodies and life work: some kids who pull wings off insects become entomologists; others become serial killers.

In the setup, is the kid repulsed by or drawn to violence? What changes that, or what increases the appeal?

How is the average inborn conscience quelled or trained? Show childhood's instinctive cruelty slowly tempered by the acquisition of empathy, often from observing and understanding the pain of pets or close friends.

A child possessed by demons is of course another story, and you could include the true self fighting to take back control or slowly giving up.

Today's justice system wrestles with appropriate trial, punishment, and rehabilitation for young killers. Explore the anguish and confusion on all sides.

EVIL TWINS

Angel on one shoulder, devil on the other? Most mythologies include a set of twins to signify this aspect of individual personalities, as well as the duality of existence: day-night, hot-cold, life-death, etc.

The twins needn't be actual twins, but there needs be some unifying foundation of ideology, profession, gender, etc. from which they can go in diverse directions, like the Bible's Cain and Abel, or Greek mythology's Prometheus (who brought fire to humans) and his brother Epimetheus (who brought Pandora's Box).

CHARACTERISTICS

Dualities, polarities, oppositions. Sense of incompleteness if alone. Envy of those who seem whole. Searching. Selectiveness... few are worthy, fewer still are chosen. Sentences could trail off, as though waiting for someone else to finish them.

A. IN ACTION

Part truth, part legend, the Mesopotamian story of arrogant, sophisticated, womanizing king Gilgamesh and Enkidu, the gentle, naïve, animal-loving man of the wilderness, is one of the oldest twin tales and buddy stories. It pits city against countryside, vain against humble. In they end they become fast friends, symbolizing the integrated personality.

In psychology, our *doppelganger* (ghost twin of self) often lives out our Shadow selves and the goal is to integrate the two.

B. IN MEDIA

In Oscar Wilde's *Portrait of Dorian Gray*, the character's evil twin is embodied in a painting that ages and shows all his sins, while he stays young and handsome, until....

Spencer Tracy and Ingrid Bergman star in the noir thriller *Dr. Jekyll and Mr. Hyde*, an excellent excursion into evil twin territory. Also see Bette Davis in *Dead Ringer* and Jeremy Irons in *Dead Ringers*. The anime movie *Spirited Away* features old lady witch twins, one evil and one kind.

In Neil Gaiman's novel *Anansi Boys*, a young man is reunited with his magical twin-self. *The Man in the Iron Mask* is about an evil king with a good twin locked away, and what happens when he's freed. In *Dave*, Kevin Kline poses the same situation around the U.S. Presidency.

In *Terminator 2*, Schwarzenegger's formerly bad Terminator is now a good guy fighting his evil twin machine. In the brutally defeatist *Fight Club*, Brad Pitt is Edward Norton's other half, but we don't find that out until the end of the film.

C. IN YOUR CREATIONS

Inner Drives Centers of Motivation – any of them, in their dualities.

Range across the sliding scale of a quality: begin your twins as indifferent slackers, then turn one into a pacifist and the other into a gung-ho soldier. Or start them both gung-ho and move one towards indifference and the other to pacifist.

If you go far enough in one direction you end up where you started. Show how one twin tries so hard to be unlike the other that they actually end up being alike.

Twins trading places makes intriguing psychological drama: the weak one becomes stronger as the strong one weakens, the shy one becomes extroverted as the show-off retreats, etc.

As in *Heat*, starring cop Al Pacino and robber Robert De Niro, show the core driver that unites two opponents. For those two, it is the intellectual challenge and the thrill of the chase.

PIRATES, REBELS, AND TRAITORS

As opposed to antiheroes who uphold some idealism, these rogues are just plain bad. If they ever had any faith in themselves or others, they've lost it. They're determined to destroy the system. Sometimes they think they're doing the right thing, but seldom for the greater good.

Some people are simply so contrary that no matter what's going on, they're going to be against it. As James Dean drawled in *Rebel Without A Cause* when asked what he was against, "What'd'ya got?" Neuroscience now locates this contrarian tendency in the brain's cingulate system; wags would say it's located at the bottom end of the digestive tract.

CHARACTERISTICS

Selfish. Disdain for the system and determination to take advantage of it. Addicted to adrenalin. Physical courage or simply not caring whether they live or die. Angry or the other extreme, indifferent. Using violence and fear to try to feel something... anything. Often self-destructive; they simply don't give a hoot about themselves or anyone else. Though spiritual teachings says there's Light inside everyone, you'd be hard pressed to find any in these people, they've done such a good job of covering it over with Darkness.

A. IN ACTION

Piracy has a long bloody history and continues today, particularly in the Indian Ocean and the South China Sea. Mercenaries fight in most wars, from Xenophon's Greeks at the Battle of Cunaxa, to German Hessians in the American Revolution, to Blackwater mercs in the early 2000s Iraq War.

One man's rebel is another's freedom fighter. We're talking about people who rebel just for the heck of it and go where the fighting is. When peace is made, they hire themselves out to fight another war.

Who gets called traitor depends on what side of the question you're on. For her actions during the Vietnam War, Jane Fonda is a heroine to anti-war protestors, but a traitor to others. Traitors in espionage agencies can expose colleagues to death and their countries to great damage. In many countries, including the U.S., the punishment for treason is death.

B. IN MEDIA

Pirate stories: Peter Pan's nemesis Captain Hook was understandably upset about losing a hand to the crocodile, but he was a rough character way before that.

Judas of the Bible's New Testament used to be an icon of the traitor until the *Gospel of Judas* was discovered. As logic has always dictated, Judas sacrificed himself and his reputation to bring about Jesus' crucifixion. Without him the whole thing couldn't have happened, so is he a traitor or a trusted aide?

Ed Harris plays an amoral rebel-for-hire in the film *Under Fire*, about photojournalists and mercenaries in Nicaragua.

Season five of the counter-terrorist TV series *24* had traitors-within-traitors nested within the plot like Russian dolls, all the way to the U.S. President. One or two thought they had noble motives, but a scratch beneath the surface of most revealed personal gain as the driver.

John Le Carre's novels and the movies made from them delve into the multifaceted world of spy and counterspy. Most James Bond films combine pirates, rebels, and traitors with lots of trick machines and glamorous girls.

C. IN YOUR CREATIONS

Inner Drives Center of Motivation – Lower Solar Plexus: selfishness, & Root: death-dealing.

Show a character's fascination with destruction; how did it begin?

Go against stereotypes and give this character an opportunity for redemption.

Show the mental path that convinced them of the meaninglessness of existence and the stupidity of humans; show how they've emotionally devolved into that give-a-sh*t grace that lets people dodge bullets and death... for a while.

Explore the addiction of action: show your character trying to settle down. How successful is that? Who does it affect, how?

Expand on the psychological idea that these types actually want to be punished.

Did you believe Anakin Skywalker's conversion to Darth Vader? Was it in him all along? Was it too contrived? Write some new pivotal scenes showing his devolvement, then tweak it for your own unique character.

BAD COP, WORSE COP

Travel to any third world country and you'll be paying extra to uniformed men for "extra service." Sometimes it's just a hassle, other times I've found the point of a gun makes the point that it's better to just pay the "tax" rather than arguing about it. From petty corruption to murder and mayhem, those who police the populace too often need policing. It's that power thing again, corrupting those who hold it.

CHARACTERISTICS

Cocky, swaggering. Love the uniforms, the guns, the medals, the machines. Competitive. Have a daddy-knows-best attitude towards the populace, but resent the powers over them. Disgusted with the bad and sad people they deal with on the streets. On constant alert, they see danger everywhere and are always ready for it.

A. IN ACTION

The bad-cop syndrome seems such an organic thing, there's usually a specific police department to deal with the downside of it. Internal Affairs is supposed to police the police, but as the film *Internal Affairs* shows, it doesn't always work.

To discourage corruption in Singapore, most public officials make more money than the U.S. Congress. Plus, any corruption is severely punished.

Those "stinking badges" from *Treasure of Sierra Madre* that the bad guys said they didn't need? A filmmaker friend traveling in the Philippines once flashed a badge to get past security hassles and onto his plane. The badge was from a Warner Brothers music video and featured Bugs Bunny. No matter, unless you look closely, a badge is a badge is a badge.

B. IN MEDIA

Our fascination with power gone bad has produced many fine bad-cop films: *Prince of the City, Internal Affairs, LA Confidential,* and *Bad Lieutenant,* where Harvey Keitel confronts redemption through a haze of addictions. In *Training Day* an idealistic young cop confronts the less-than-ethical methods his mentor uses to fight evil.

The Oscar-winning *Crash* is a window on the slippery slope of good cop, bad cop, worse cop.

TV series dealing with this archetype are exceptionally popular, such as the *Law and Order* franchise, *NYPD Blue*, and *The Wire*.

Prison guards are stationary cops, wading in the muck of prisoners' failure, hatred, and frustration. *The Shawshank Redemption*, *The Green Mile*, and *Monster's Ball* offer portrayals of this type of cop.

C. IN YOUR CREATIONS

Inner Drives Center of Motivation - Lower Solar Plexus: personal power over others, & Sacral: sex, money, and fear as indulgences and as power tools over others.

Greed and distorted personal power have corrupted these characters. Show us this process anywhere along the line and you'll be tapping into a major human tendency.

Do a ride-along with your local cops. Visit a jail or prison.

Show the progress of a cop going from initial compassion and a sense of order to disappointment and hopelessness.

Use order or the lack thereof in her personal life to either contrast or support the sense of order in the cop's professional life.

Take us back to the early times when they lacked power and decided to never feel that way again. What roads to power did they not go down and why?

Show how keeping-up-with-the-Joneses can become a downward spiral of illegal and immoral actions.

BUMBLERS

One reason the Mystery Schools are secret is because a little knowledge is a dangerous thing. You don't turn the steering wheel over to a toddler, give a machine gun to an eight year old, or hand the security code for the nukes to the physics freshman. Well, some do... and that makes for tense stories, since chaos is bound to ensue.

Bumblers can be a foil for the hero, a sharp contrast to his abilities. They're also an immediate opportunity for the hero to demonstrate tolerance and helpfulness, thus enhancing his esteem.

CHARACTERISTICS

Cocky. Self-assured. Entitled. Doesn't listen to others. Brags. Looks down on others. Blind to their own mistakes.

Cheery to the point of nausea, helpful to the point of harmful.

Or the other extreme: shy, inept, tries to hide, mumbles, fearful, clumsy.

A. IN ACTION

In business theory this is the Peter Principle, where a person rises to their level of incompetence.

Empires are often headed by Bumblers who're puppets of the real power players. It's common in dynasties where a bloodline rather than brain power gets you the office. Cleopatra's younger brother is a tragic example.

Manipulators keep their own hands clean by getting Bumblers to pull the trigger and be the fall guy for all sorts of badness, from simple extortion to assassinations, as some suppose with Lee Harvey Oswald killing President Kennedy and Sirhan Sirhan killing Robert Kennedy.

Sometimes sins of omission are just as bad as sins of commission. Those who do nothing and allow Evil to thrive are judged just as guilty as those who help it along.

In casting, this is the Producer's Girlfriend factor — the well-connected person who really can't perform.

B. IN MEDIA

Situation comedies rely on this type for plot drivers: their mistakes set up the situation, their bumbling supplies the comedy. The *Dilbert* cartoon strip pits competent Dilbert against an office full of Bumblers; Bumbler bosses Ricky Gervais and Steve Carell of *The Office* TV series try everyone's patience.

Fox TV *24*'s superagent Jack Bauer ices loads of unwary Bumblers every episode. These people are usually led by others to think they're doing the wrong thing for the right reason, such as nuking LA to make us safer.

Mickey Mouse in *Fantasia's* "Sorcerer's Apprentice," Billy Bob Thornton's *Bad Santa*, River Phoenix in *My Own Private Idaho*, and Stan Laurel of the old comedy team Laurel and Hardy are variants of this archetype. They turn ineffectiveness into an art and bumble their way to comedy or tragedy. They're fascinating the way a train wreck is fascinating. Peter Falk's Detective Columbo used this archetype as a cover for his cleverness.

C. IN YOUR CREATIONS

Inner Drives Center of Motivation – Throat: faulty, never thinking things through, & Lower Solar Plexus: unwarranted confidence, or wimpy lack of confidence.

Follow Murphy's Law: Anything that can go wrong, will.

Why do these people think they're so great? Who lied to them? Their mommas? A yes-man?

What happens when their incompetencies are revealed? Do they get angry? Deny it? Collapse?

Show a wimp rising to the occasion. Can they stay there after the emergency, or is the power too strong for them?

Show what happens if others refuse to enable a Bumbler. If in combat, will they die? If in business, go broke?

Have your heroine develop a doofus detector (instinct, pointed questions, trials, etc.) over the course of the story so she eventually learns to avoid Bumblers.

DICTATORS, TYRANTS, AND CULT LEADERS

These people are alpha male types gone mad and really bad. Societies in weakness or disarray often look to a strong man (sometimes woman) for leadership. Herd instinct kicks in and an individual rises to meet the need.

CHARACTERISTICS

Charismatic. Clever. Proud. Arrogant. Insensitive. Intuitive. Exude a sense confidence and power. They'll lock gazes with you (you're the deer in the headlights) and speak hypnotically. Often sexually voracious. Ruthless and slightly, or maybe totally, mad.

A. IN ACTION

Read history, watch The History Channel, and check out current events.

After the first Gulf War, many wondered why the first President Bush left Saddam in power. One of the reasons is now painfully obvious. Power, like nature, abhors a vacuum. A dictator is a stabilizing force, and it's much easier to cut deals with focused brutality than with anarchy.

Cult leaders are like dark whirlpools, fascinating, hypnotic, and deadly. They usually control their followers through sex, money, and fear, using the latter to intimidate them into giving them the first two. At Jim Jones' People's Temple in Guyana you also got to drink the Kool-Aid™, kill your kids, and die.

Creating a climate of fear requires making examples, so brutal tortures and deaths frequently surround these people, be it heads on poles, "disappeared" family, or massacres of entire settlements.

B. IN MEDIA

Read Percy Bisshe Shelley's classic poem *Ozymandius* about the fate of a great tyrant.

Some see these types as emissaries of the Dark Brotherhood, here to promote fear and helplessness. Many fantasy stories, particularly from Asia, offer fascinating theories on how they came about and how to get rid of them.

Shakespeare's *Richard III* is a wretched but very effective dictator, particularly as played by Ian McKellan in the 1995 movie.

An excellent study of this type of villain is Ian Richardson again, playing unscrupulous British Prime Minister Francis Urguhart (F.U.) in Michael Dobbs's novels and the BBC series *House of Cards*.

In *The Last King of Scotland* Forest Whitaker portrays the charismatic mad dictator of Uganda, Idi Amin. Based on the Joseph Conrad novel *Heart of Darkness*, Marlon Brando's Colonel Kurtz in *Apocalypse Now* is a good man gone really bad from too much power.

C. IN YOUR CREATIONS

Inner Drives Center of Motivation - dropped Ajnas: consummate control dropped to corrupt power-mongering.

A virgin carrying a bag of gold could walk safely from one end of the realm to another in Genghis Khan's empire. What can your tyrant truly be proud of? The trains run on time (Mussolini's Italy), everyone has medical care (Castro's Cuba), or racial and religious persecution is forbidden (Lee Kuan Yew's Singapore). And at what price to the people?

Kermit Roosevelt helped put the Shah of Iran in power; there are great stories yet to be written about that, as well as U.S. manipulation of dictators during the Cold War. See the chapter on "Groupthink Stinks."

If you're creating speculative fiction, where does the tyrant fit in to the Dark Brotherhood's big picture? What's the ultimate goal? Does she know, or is she a pawn?

How can your protagonist take out the tyrant without another one filling the vacuum? Does she start at the bottom and get the people to rise up? Start in the middle and convert those who benefit somewhat from cooperation with the oppressor but pay a high price for it? Convince the rulers that a change would benefit them? How?

What was this person like as a baby? Would they have grown up to be this bad regardless? Show us at least three pivotal steps.

MAD SCIENTISTS

The *devas* of ideas and inventions have taken over these villains at the expense of their humanity and common sense. The world of the mind is fascinating, mathematics has been called the language of god, and discovery is thrilling. But Asimov's rules for robots to the contrary, machines have no conscience and scientific innovations have been known to harm humans.

CHARACTERISTICS

Smart. Very smart. Very very smart. Narrowly focused on their own discipline. Visionary, yet short-sighted. Fascinated with the physical world. Sometimes bordering on psychopathic, they truly do not understand emotions. Meticulous, measured, sometimes jealous of their inventions, but ready to techie-talk forever.

A. IN ACTION

Some people object to scientific progress on religious grounds; others want it to proceed slowly enough to reveal the downside before we're in too deep. Mad scientists don't give a flip about either, that's why we have Bioethics. Scientists go through a peer review process before publishing in official journals so other scientists can check their work for accuracy and applicability.

Real scientific innovation usually happens in secret government labs and then spins off into commercial uses: global positioning systems, digital cinema, the Internet, and who knows what else is in the pipeline?

B. IN MEDIA

Legend has it the fall of Atlantis was caused by proud scientists misusing their crystal power technology. In the Old Testament, arrogant architects of the Tower of Babel, intending to reach heaven, were foiled when Yahweh confused their languages; rather like when NASA used inches on one part of a Mars lander and metric on another... oops.

Every sci-fi B movie you've ever seen. Dr. Frankenstein was a scientist; look what happened there.

In *Terminator, Battlestar Galactica, The Matrix, I, Robot,* and *A.I.,* the problems originated when scientists took machines too far towards artificial intelligence. The *Dune* novels take place centuries after computers have failed and human mentats do it all with sheer brainpower.

In *Antitrust*, Ryan Phillippe plays a young computer genius drawn into the megalomania plan of a Bill Gates-like Tim Robbins determined to create a global satellite system, no matter what it costs in money or in lives.

Nazi doctors, such as the sadistic dentist Laurence Olivier in *Marathon Man*, set a low standard for gruesome curiosity.

C. IN YOUR CREATIONS

Inner Drives Center of Motivation - Throat Center: intellect, invention, fascination with science and technology.

Show how your scientist has different approaches and uses for hardware, software, and wetware (brainpower).

Imagine the next-step-plus-one from a particular technology and have your character build it. Cell phones embedded in wrists and ears, large flexible TV screens you can unroll and hang on walls, your own stem cells turned into a personalized health tonic, genetically engineered chimeras (animals made of different species: lion-eagle, human-horse, anteater-pitbull).

Your modern scientist could discover that seemingly primitive practices might be remnants of high technologies: herbal medicine = pharmacology; sky myths = astronomy; migration myths = plate tectonics; chant and dance = stimulation of certain brain regions, etc.

Subscribe to *Science News, Scientific American,* and *Skeptic* for general information and provocative mad scientist story ideas.

You have to break eggs to make omelets. What's your mad scientist willing to sacrifice for science: their position, reputation, a child, the planet?

Everybody needs a Rosebud (the sled from *Citizen Kane*). What's the tender moment or childhood token that could weaken this antagonist?

PYCHOPATHS, PEDOPHILES, AND SERIAL KILLERS

Science has taken a lot of the onus out of madness by revealing how chemicals in the brain influence our feelings and actions. But rather than seeing them as engines needing a tune-up, we mostly still view these people as vicious, irredeemable monsters.

CHARACTERISTICS

No conscience. No empathy. No connection with any normal human emotions. Robotic. Or, a hyper-activation of selected emotions such as rage, lust, or cruelty. Study psychological profiles to better understand these types. Sometimes very charming but having the "evil twin" aspect at work when they kill.

A. IN ACTION

History reveals these people sometimes as rulers, sometimes as aberrations reviled by society, but always present in every time and place. Everyone knew Roman Emperor Nero was an evil nutcase, and in *Farewell Brave Babylon* Saddam Hussein's pilot recounts that he sensed pure evil the first time he met the Iraqi dictator.

People who've been in combat sometimes admit to having felt these sensations coursing through them as they fought for survival, but their feelings are temporary.

Brain science and psychology note a lack of brain wiring in psychopaths and similar offenders. There's a broad spectrum of guilt, but apparently some people simply don't feel any. Then there are those who feel guilt, remorse, and revulsion but are powerless to stop themselves. With some notable exceptions, most of these types are men, which leads to all sorts of speculation about "testosterone poisoning."

B. IN MEDIA

History and horror films have given us Freddie Krueger of *Nightmare on Elm Street*, Jason of *Friday the 13th*, England's Jack the Ripper, Hannibal Lecter, Ed Guin, and Norman Bates of - *Psycho*.

Sometimes these people think they're doing the world a favor by wiping out bad people, like Kevin Spacey in *Se7en*. Sometimes they're mindless zombies like in *Night of the Living Dead*. In the films *Jacob's Ladder* and *Serenity*, it was government experiments gone bad that created the mad killers.

An interesting study in paedophilia and incest is to try and find the dividing line between inappropriate affection and criminal lust. Why is Brooke Shields' sexual experience in *Pretty Baby* art, but Leland Palmer's love of his daughter in *Twin Peaks* is criminal? Watch Stanley Kubrick's *A Clockwork Orange* for a troubling close-up of violent sociopaths.

C. IN YOUR CREATIONS

Inner Drives Center Motivation – Root: death, killing, survival.

Because it's hard for ordinary people to understand how psychopaths function, show us the background incidents that stifled their development, shut down their emotions, or damaged their brains. Not to excuse them but to add conflict to the situation... can you blame someone who doesn't know any better or who truly can't help themselves?

Confront the legal dilemma of whether or not to incarcerate people who are insane.

If a person truly believes they're meant to wipe out corruption, might they be right?

If you could rewire our brains, how would you do it? What would result?

Are some people just born bad? If so, why? What do you do with them as a parent, teacher, friend, colleague, law officer?

CONCLUSION

There are all sorts of fascinating and dramatic ways to be bad. Your unique insights and elaborations on these characters will enrich the various archetypes.

7.
GROUPTHINK STINKS

+ Stereotypes, racism, classism

+ Cultural clashes

+ Kids and cliques

+ Child warriors and child workers

+ Vandals, Goths, Golden Hordes

+ Soldiers of God

+ Organized religion

+ Organized crime

+ Corporate corruption

+ Secret societies and shadow governments

+ Big Brothers and bureaucracies

+ Evil empires

+ War, huh, what is it good for?

"If everybody else was jumping off a bridge, I suppose you'd want to do it, too?!" an exasperated mother replies to her child's outrageous request. The child's answer of course is, "Yes!"

Groupthink drives one of the biggest industries on the planet — fashion, and its ancillaries diet and fitness. Political correctness is a bow to ethnic groupthink. Many armed conflicts are symptoms of groupthink gone bad. Lines of lemmings jumping off Arctic cliffs and rows of soldiers marching in lockstep signify the downside of groupthink. Groupthink is so prevalent we even measure time and the progress of a culture by it, using terms such as *zeitgeist* (the spirit of an age, when everyone thought such-and-thus) or "The Age of Reason," or "The Hippie Era." Such monolithic backgrounds can provide looming opposition for your heroine's individuality.

There are different kinds of groupthink.

1) Hive-herd-tribal instinct. It causes us to huddle in times of danger, to shun the "other," and to cluster into strata, cliques, and castes. It is our animal nature.

2) Seemingly rational thinking. A group of individuals makes decisions contrary to their own needs, which supposedly fulfills the needs of the group, e.g. soldiers in combat giving their own lives for others, for principles, or beliefs.

3) Forced groupthink. An individual or small cluster of people impose their will on a much larger group through the use of force, fear, propaganda, desire, faith, or any combination thereof. Murderous military dictatorships and repressive religions fall into this category.

These can be powerful sources of opposition for your protagonists, whether they're struggling to rise above conformity ("I just gotta be me!"), trying to alert others about the danger of their ways ("I got a bad feeling about this"), or trying to foment rebellion against oppressors ("Soylent Green is people!", or "I'm mad as hell and I'm not going to take it anymore!").

STEREOTYPES, RACISM, CLASSISM

Evil is often a good that's been held onto for too long. Our animal nature and the isolation of primitive peoples has left remnants of what used to protect us — fear of "the other" who might carry diseases for which we have no immunity. To preserve itself, the herd kills or abandons runts, the injured, the weak.

Science now pinpoints the location in the brain that recognizes and recoils at "the other," and species separation is so strong we still marvel over stories of cheetahs adopting baby baboons or pigs and turtles forming friendships.

As our higher minds and more open hearts embrace differences within the unity of all life, our primitive survival instinct still emerges in horrific ways.

A. IN ACTION

Throughout history, invaders label natives as less than human, even if the natives have built extensive cities, amazing temples, and sophisticated societies. Hey, if your weapons are bigger and more effective, you're obviously a better species, and those "others" are unworthy of living except as slaves.

Recent American foreign policy has been accused of selective salvation: we went into white European Bosnia to stop genocide, but not into black African Rwanda or Darfur.

In India, lower castes make up 80% of the populace, though the Untouchables have made significant progress in claiming rights and access to avenues of self-improvement.

Thought processes are not immune to persecution either, as seen in the execution of intellectuals in the killing fields of Khmer Rouge, China's Cultural Revolution, Nazis burning books, religious fundamentalists banning books or killing authors, and repressive regimes exterminating the press.

B. IN MEDIA

Othello, Heart of Darkness, Heat of the Sun, Upstairs-Downstairs, Gunga Din, Sharp's Rifles, The Raj Quartet, Fahrenheit 451, In the

Heat of the Night, Nine to Five, The Killing Fields, Hotel Rwanda, Before the Rain, In My Country, Driving Miss Daisy, Crash, Lord of the Flies, Lost. The operas "Lakme" and "Aida."

That early *Star Trek* episode where the people with the left side of their faces are white and the other black persecuted those who were just the opposite. Dr. Seuss' *Sneetches.*

C. IN YOUR CREATIONS

Inner Drives Center of Motivation - Root & Lower Solar Plexus

This is such an instinctual drive that your otherwise high-minded characters could be struck at a gut level, then realize what they're doing, and logic their way out of the reaction. People unsure of their own identity tend to define themselves against the "other."

Be sure to show us the distinctions and some background as to how it came about. To deepen drama, show the value of separatism to a character or group, even if we don't agree with their reasoning.

Even if your character succeeds in breaking down barriers in this story, keep tension in the resolution by showing that it's not a time-less global cure.

Show actions counter to the stereotype, but also show why the stereotype exists, correctly or incorrectly. Until we understand a thing, we can't defeat or dissolve it.

CULTURAL CLASHES

Traditions, taboos, and superstitions spawn practices seen as per-fectly natural to local practitioners but often horrifying to others. They include oppressive polygamy (multiple wives), genital muti-lation, cannibalism, ritual sacrifice, and the like. Being local, they often arise to meet perceived societal needs. Being human, they often give sanction to our dark Dweller.

A. IN ACTION

European Christian colonizers were appalled by the nudity and seeming promiscuousness of native people; the indigenous people were appalled by the cannibalistic rites of Christian communion — eating the body and drinking blood of their god?!

In some African tribes, widows undergo sexual cleansing to prevent haunting by the husband's ghost. Each village has a designated Cleanser to have sex with widows. It's a job-for-life and generally considered a dirty job, but somebody's gotta do it.

Conflicts over veiling of women continue worldwide as tribal groupthink clashes with modernity. In Czarist Russia, and recently in Afghanistan, men were put to death for the length of their beards.

B. IN MEDIA

In some African and Islamic cultures apparently fearful of female sexual power, young women are circumcised to ensure fidelity and marriageability. Other females perpetuate this practice of mutilating their daughters, often as babies, so they can fit into the local groupthink. *Beyond Honor* shows this in contemporary Southern California.

In Deepa Mehta's film *Water* an innocent child bride is exiled to the widows' compound. Less brutal than *suttee*, where widows are encouraged to burn alive on their husband's funeral pyre, it still allows the family to claim her property yet avoid supporting her.

The TV series *Big Love* is about polygamy among American Mormons.

A turning point in *Braveheart* occurs when Wallace's sweetheart is subjected to *le droit signeur*, the right of the local lord to deflower all the virgins under his rule on their wedding night, a practice which may have been an old system to keep bloodlines strong and ensure familial loyalty.

Ritual cannibalism is a mystical way to incorporate the energy (*deva*) of the eatee (you are who you eat). Greek myths track the cursed Atriedes family through generations of tragedy, begun when Tantalus cooked his son Pelops into a stew for the gods. Shakespeare followed with *Titus Andronicus* and Julie Taymor directed the movie of that play.

C. IN YOUR CREATIONS

Inner Drives Center of Motivation - Lower Solar Plexus, Sacral, & Root: all tribal, separatist motivators.

Have someone in your story explore the core practical intent of the practice. Was it originally to protect women from unwanted sexual attention, to protect men's egos from unwanted sexual demands, to save poor villagers the burden of caring for widows, to reiterate the group customs and maintain order, to protect an insular tribe from outsiders' germs, etc? Dig beneath the superstitions and get to the evolutionary psychology behind the acts. Why did this continue? What has changed? Can it be discarded now?

This is a perfect setup for a fish-out-of-water story.

Add an ironic twist as the horrified hero eventually sees some echo of the practice he condemns at work within his own system: cannibalism and the Christian Eucharist; *le droit signeur* and stomping the glass at a Jewish wedding; Aborigine circumcision rites and freshman hazing, etc.

One value of war and conquest can be to shatter old beliefs and move culture forward. Focus on a couple of characters and show differences in how they deal with these challenges: abolition of slavery, women's freedoms, etc.

Initiation rites for moving into puberty often involve trials and pain to prove one can mold into groupthink. Some say American boys, deprived of initiation rites, don't know how to grow up and become men. Create rites, besides gang initiations, that might accomplish this.

KIDS AND CLIQUES

After the family, a child's next exposure to groupthink is the playground. Teen angst is triggered by being thought "uncool," and some teens start pulling triggers because they're cruelly shut out of a group.

A. IN ACTION

Bullying is a huge problem in almost every country and culture. In a bit of generalization, kids in Japan commit suicide over it, while kids in America pick up guns and kill others because of it.

B. IN MEDIA

Mean Girls, Heathers, My Life as a Dog, The Breakfast Club, Grease, Hair Spray, Legally Blonde, and *Swing Kids* where Nazism strains young Germans' friendships.

C. IN YOUR CREATIONS

Inner Drives Center of Motivation - Lower Solar Plexus: the self, boundaries. On the down side: separatism, cliques, hatred of "other".

Use dress codes, jargon, signals of any sort that divide people into "this" versus "that" or "them" versus "us."

Start with someone from the outside wanting to be in the group. Have an initiation — gruesome, icky, or cruel. Show your character resisting, then overcoming her natural anathema and succumbing against her better judgment.

Show a former friend being hurt because of your character's actions. Does the character change, or not?

Are the rewards of belonging to the clique enough for the character? Is he totally absorbed into the group? Does he harbor some
individuality? Might he step away?

Show some reflection of this in the grown-up world, in history,
myth, or media so that we can see where it could all lead to tears,
even if in your story it does not.

CHILD WARRIORS AND
CHILD WORKERS

Some observe that adolescence is a modern invention and until
the early part of the 20th century in western Europe and America,
children have always worked and have often gone to war.

Amnesty International reports tens of thousands of child soldiers in
conflicts raging around the globe, particularly in Africa. Kidnapped
kids are usually forced to kill someone else, using horror and guilt
to make them obedient. Human empathy needs to be hardwired
into the brain by age eight, so many are lost to any redemption.

Many trade treaties regulate against goods made by children.
Public awareness about fair labor practices has improved the situation somewhat, but it's hard to enforce subcontractors in remote
locales or overcrowded cities.

Children are a huge sector in the sex worker industry, often sold
by poverty-stricken parents unaware of their fates. In economic
terms, until the demand goes away, the ruthless and the helpless
will furnish the supply side of this damaging market.

A. IN ACTION

The Children's Crusade of 1212 saw 20,000 children marching
through Europe headed to the Holy Land to free Jerusalem from the
Moslems. Many died on the way and many were sold into slavery.

Many Islamic terrorists are trained in radical *madrassas*, schools which teach distorted versions of the *Koran*, rabid politics, and little else. Young soldiers indoctrinated in this groupthink easily strap on suicide bombs.

The U.N. estimates one million children are forced into prostitution each year. The Internet has proliferated and globalized child porn.

Child protection laws and increased awareness so far seem unable to stem the rising tide of child abuse in soldiering, commerce, and the sex trade.

B. IN MEDIA

Little Miss Sunshine offers a poignant perspective on the sexualization of very young girls, as do *Pretty Baby*, and *Taxi Driver*.

Even if kids escape the military, it's hard to make them fit for regular society. Mr. Eko in the TV series *Lost* followed this cruel path, but fashions a shaky redemption by masquerading as a priest. A couple of former African boy-soldiers have written biographies; some documentaries cover this as well.

Charles Dickens often wrote about exploited children, and the 12th-century Children's Crusade spawned many novels.

C. IN YOUR CREATIONS

Inner Drives Center of Motivation - Sacral & Root. For most kids, it's about doing whatever it takes to survive, whether it's sex or soldiering.

Show as many facets of the situation as you can without cluttering up the story: the parents or lack thereof, the economic pressures, the desperation and madness of homegrown armies and militias, the training schools.

Expose the background drivers of government, businesses, local customs, superstitions, social pressures, etc.

Illustrate end products tainted by this perverse groupthink: blood diamonds, cheap goods at big box stores, sex tourism.

Show differences in how kids adapt to the stark situations. Who bonds, who stays aloof? Show how differently they recover, or not. Who seeks love and redemption? Who just wants to hurt others?

Cautionary tales show the consequences of actions. Will the boy soldier become a Richard the Lionheart or a Hitler? Will the young prostitute die of AIDS and abuse or become an advocate for others? Why does one go one way and one the other?

VANDALS, GOTHS, GOLDEN HORDES

There is something in the nature of man that loves a good battle, and if need be, we'll travel far and wide in search of it. Though it's a brutal way to do it, sometimes the God of War must be credited with stirring up gene pools and cultures through rape, pillage, and looting. Soldiers are the carriers of ideas, customs, arts, crafts, and religions, as well as genes.

In groups such as this, there's usually a strong, charismatic figure at the head, and very strong male bonding amongst the followers. Soldiers often profess love for the leader bordering on worship and Romance with a capital "R". Strict codes of behavior and rough justice keep the rowdies working together for their common purpose. Fierce loyalty often ensues. Sycophants can flourish, and the juggling for succession offers opportunity for dark intrigue.

Uniforms, body markings, special languages, high signs, codes, and war stories are valued. Violence is the watchword. Honor is a valued commodity and any slight must be repaid with a duel to the death or just an outright vengeance slaying. A version of this gang-type boy bonding is what militaries try to instill in boot camp.

A. IN ACTION

Genghis Khan and the 13th-century Mongol Hordes; Attila the Hun and his guys sweeping across eastern Europe; the Goths, Visigoths, and Vandals who helped bring down the once-mighty Roman Empire; Vikings marauding across northern Europe and America; warlords in feudal China; and the more formal but still deadly Samurai of the Japanese Shogunate. And for girls, the Amazon female warriors.

B. IN MEDIA

Alexander, Troy, Shogun, The Last Samurai, Xena: Warrior Princess, and the *Hercules '90s* TV series, *Taps,* and *Pathfinder,* about the Vikings.

C. IN YOUR CREATIONS

Inner Drives Center of Motivation - Lower Solar Plexus: power, & Root: sheer survival.

Show how strong LSP motivations create the honor thing and tight bonding, excluding others.

Play up the internal competition between guys, and for the leader's favor.

Some members should be motivated by idealism and want to make a difference, to right political wrongs. Others are just in it for the fighting and the booty. Use that contrast for conflict among the warriors.

What happens when a horde guy gets old? Or wants to settle down?

SOLDIERS OF GOD

A real problem with religions claiming to hold the Truth is that they tend to be exclusive, and exclusivity often leads to extermination of the "other." History is soggy from the blood of forced religious conversions. Some sword wielders may have been true believers, but most crusades are orchestrated by power mongers, empire builders, and ubermerchants.

Also, some people just want to fight and hurt and kill; a religious reason that promises rewards in the afterlife works just fine.

People who don't think or feel. If you can control their emotions, you can control their actions. Beliefs are the easiest way to control people, starting with fear then offering hope. Use both (hell and heaven), and you've got 'em hooked.

A. IN ACTION

From Homer's god-guided Greeks to modern Iraq's warring Sunnis and Shias, militaries often appeal to a belief in a god and drape their campaigns in the cloak of righteousness.

Anthropologists believe the Aztec, Maya, Toltec, and Inca often went to war to obtain human sacrifices for their religious rituals. Had they just taken too literally the order to "lift your hearts unto god"?

Then there're the Crusades between Christendom and Islam, which spread from Arabia by sword, as well as hearts and minds. Religious wars in Europe formally began with Martin Luther and the Protestant Reformation in 1517. Spanish and Portuguese conquistadors plundered the New World for the Catholic Church. Hindu-Muslim conflicts in India flared when the British Empire left in 1948 and still rage today.

B. IN MEDIA

The Old Testament is full of stories of zealot warriors invading and conquering the land their god promised them.

Kingdom of Heaven, Joan of Arc, Queen Margot, The Mission, Luther, Apocalypto.

A culture's foundation myths often include deity-blessed or deity-led wars to conquer or defend the homeland.

C. IN YOUR CREATIONS

Inner Drives Center of Motivation - Lower Solar Plexus: personal power and small-group bonding, & Aspirational Solar Plexus: idealism.

Uneducated, unquestioning people are easiest led by belief. Give your character some learning, some exposure to other systems, and precipitate a crisis of faith.

Have the deity fail, and the usual explanations don't satisfy. Characters at loose ends after a loss of faith and meaning are fascinating.

Where is deity on the battlefield? Both sides often pray to the same deity for victory, so why bother to train or prepare if it's all up to a deity anyway? God helps those who help themselves, but both sides did that and one still lost. This line of thinking can drive your characters nuts and hurl them out to secularism or pull them back into the nonthinking shell of blind faith.

ORGANIZED RELIGION

Social science notes that when a culture shifts from just having a local shaman to having a priestly caste, it's expanding in both size and sophistication. Order is kept by religious proscriptions: It's much more efficient to implant a little policeman (morals) inside everyone than to patrol the streets 24/7.

Karl Marx said "Religion is the opium of the people." Religion also controls the money through tithing, tributes, and manipulations of trade.

Religions offer inspiration to beauty, compel us to behave with compassion, and offer pathways to union with higher power, usually through manipulation of our senses via art, music, postures, chants, sensory deprivation, or stimulation. They've promoted marvelous progress in education, art, and health care, but let's take a look at the damage.

A. IN ACTION

Nobody expects the Spanish Inquisition, notes a cleverly scathing Monty Python skit, but religious persecution has been the order of the day since religion was invented.

Crazed mobs of Christians rejecting logic and learning in the 4th century CE rampaged through Alexandria, Egypt, tore apart the great female philosopher and mathematician Hypatia, and torched the city's magnificent library, destroying thousands of years of collected wisdom in the name of their religion.

Cardinal Richelieu, Prime Minister of France in the early 1600s (*The Three Musketeers*), saw religion as an instrument of state, and believed that ends justify means. He bloodily defeated the Huguenot religious resistance (*Queen Margot*).

Jesuit missionaries of the Colonial era Catholic Church went around the globe preparing the way for trade and military incursions (*The Mission*). Contemporary Liberation Theology in Latin America and the Philippines often pits populist priests and nuns against the party line of the Catholic Church, as well as the tyrannical regimes they preach against.

Four hundred years of Church-sanctioned witch trials in Europe executed thousands of accused Satan worshipers, mostly women. See more at *www.TheSpanishInquisition.ow.*

Religious systems that completely deny our natural impulses are asking for trouble. It's one thing to suggest austerities for a training period like Hindu, Buddhist, and Native American systems do; but a lifetime of going against human nature often causes backlash, as in pedophile Catholic priest scandals.

B. IN MEDIA

The Da Vinci Code, The Name of the Rose, The Mission, The Seventh Seal, The Three Musketeers, Queen Margot, The Jewel in the Crown, The Exorcist, The Scarlet Letter, Resurrection, Leap of Faith, Dogma.

The Bene Gesserit Order in Frank Herbert's *Dune* novels is a feminine version of the Jesuits, spreading prophecies via religion to pave the way for expansion across the universe.

Paul Scott's rich *Raj Quartet* novels and the BBC series based on them, *The Jewel in the Crown*, chronicle the 1948 separation of India into Hindu and Muslim states, still at war today as India and Pakistan.

Neal Stephenson's *Baroque Cycle* novels swirl around Europe's religious wars, when science first challenged the Church's control via Isaac Newton, Robert Hooke, Gottfried Leibniz, the Royal Society, and Freemasonry.

C. IN YOUR CREATIONS

Inner Drives Center of Motivation - Solar Plexus, Lower & Aspirational.

The tragedy of the Dark Side in religion is that its supposed purpose is to enlighten. Rather than just the evil stuff, be sure to show a range of characters: true believers who actually do good (Mother Theresa), the self-deluded (TV evangelists), the psychopathic (Torquemada, Silas in *Da Vinci Code*), perverts taking advantage of the system, as well as regular people who find comfort and inspiration in the rituals and faith.

Religious faith is anathema to the atheist, bemusing to the agnostic. For true believers, it brooks no questions and entertains no doubts. Show this disparity between the points of view and have your characters passionately question each other.

If you are promoting a belief system in your story, give us something to contrast it with: some other system, curious people, lapsed believers, hypocrites. Remember that religions are man-made systems that preserve and promote both enlightened spiritual truths and human flaws such as repression and control.

Many nonbelievers find many religions' resistance to logic, broad education, and individual freedoms a mark of backward, frightened people controlled by cynical leaders. For dramatic conflict, show that this is not always the case: within the suppression, show creative outpouring; within the manipulation, show actual spiritual connection; within mindless devotion, show sharp intelligence that believes nonetheless.

The Dark Night of the Soul by Saint John captures the pain of spiritual disconnect. Have a character wandering and angry, or sorrowful, once they've lost faith and must rearrange their entire worldview, like Neo awakening in *The Matrix*.

Most of all, show the power of faith and how it can be tragically misused by the Dark Side, whether Dwellers on the Threshold or that scary Dark Brotherhood.

ORGANIZED CRIME

Some argue that organized crime simply brings order to otherwise chaotic activities that will happen regardless. Rather than random uncontrolled extortion, prostitution, gambling, political corruption, vengeance, drink, and drugs, a crime lord imposes order on the indulgence of our Dark Side.

During Prohibition in America (1920-1933), possession or drinking of alcohol was not against the law, but the manufacture, sale, or transport of it was, kind of like marijuana now. People making millions selling illegal drugs certainly don't want it legalized.

Maybe gangs are the human evolution of hunting packs and will always be with us, since young men are like wolf pups and demand alpha male control. Street gangs also offer a sense of belonging to immigrant and underprivileged youth, as well as a captive workforce for adult gangs.

A. IN ACTION

Mafias, Japanese Yakuza, Chinese Tongs, and street gangs embody this group archetype. Though supposedly operating outside the law, most of these groups are either tolerated or aided and abetted by some aspects of the legal system.

Organizations often have their own complex legal systems. Sometimes scores are settled in all-out gang wars that cause tragic collateral damage. Sometimes they're settled by one-on-one to-the-death combat in a sports ring setting, with each side's champion quite willing to become the honored blood sacrifice to keep the local peace.

B. IN MEDIA

In *The Godfather*, Don Corleone argues against bringing in dope; he's afraid of the wrong element and how drugs might bring down the people they both prey on and protect.

West Side Story, Air America, The Untouchables, The Godfather, The Seven Samurai, The Magnificent Seven, The French Connection, The Sopranos, Yakuza, Black Rain, Warriors, Colors, Bound (this stylish lesbo-mobster romp was the Wachowski brothers' first feature), *City of God, Scarface, LA Confidential, Boondock Saints, Traffic, Deadwood, A History of Violence,* and on the funny side *Prizzi's Honor, Married to the Mob,* and *Get Shorty.*

C. IN YOUR CREATIONS

Inner Drives Center of Motivation - Lower Solar Plexus: power, greed, exclusivity.

Show collateral damage on kids, women, property, and social order (*The Seven Samurai*). Show how fear paralyzes creativity. Show how drugs and prostitution squelch self esteem; how getting high keeps you down. It's no coincidence that the world's slums are huge drug markets; think what would happen if all those disaffected people sobered up and took action!

America has an odd attraction to the Mafia: perhaps a leftover adolescent desire for a strong father figure and the camaraderie of fellow warriors. Show what happens when someone "grows up" and wants out.

Show how a gang gets started to fill some societal need for protection, distraction, release. Give us a "gateway" incident; have some warn against it, others pooh-pooh it as harmless.

If there wasn't a market for what the mob was selling, they'd be out of business. How might that play out?

For an exotic setting for your mob story, explore the island of Macau, the "Vegas of the Far East."

CORPORATE CORRUPTION

Many conspiracy theories cast big business, big pharmaceuticals, big energy, and big banking as the power tools of the Dark Brotherhood, intent on enslaving and torturing mankind. Look at the disparity of wealth, number of people on legal drugs, climate change, and overwhelming credit card debt in America alone and you might just agree.

For centuries corporations have been considered artificial persons with all the legal rights and protections of natural persons.

Basically, it's the creation of a *deva*, with all that implies about an archetype. Unlike Japanese 200-year plans or native Americans' 7th-generation consideration, U.S. corporations concentrate on the quarterly report, seriously diminishing vision and awareness of consequences.

Whether it's a collective Dweller on the Threshold or a tool of the Dark Brotherhood, the more you know about the motivations and machinations of the corporation, the more intriguing your corporate villain can be.

A. IN ACTION

In the Opium Wars of the mid 1800s the British East India Company forced opium onto the Chinese market to equalize their balance of trade. It's how the Brits got Hong Kong.

A major background driver in *The Pirates of the Caribbean* movies is sea trade by colonial corporations. Piracy today is a huge corporate problem in the Indian Ocean and South China Sea. Much U.S. military and covert operations in Central and Latin America is credited to protection of U.S. corporate interests.

As water becomes more precious than oil, multinational corporations are trying to gain control over water supplies in many underdeveloped countries, forcing locals to pay for a local resource they've gotten free for eons.

Besides problems from untested drugs, also research Three Mile Island, Chernobyl, and the Union Carbide Bhopal incidents to see how corporations try to protect themselves from blame.

B. IN MEDIA

The Mission, Chinatown, Rollerball, Three Mile Island, Brazil, Wall Street, Silkwood, The Insider, Erin Brokovich, The Constant Gardener, and *The Day After Tomorrow* center on corporate malfeasance. The De Beers company controls the diamond trade, except for blood diamonds, mined in violence-torn African countries to finance local conflicts.

A Dangerous Man: Lawrence After Arabia, starring Ralph Fiennes, dramatizes the post-WWI division of Middle East oil fields among England, France, and the U.S., including the creation of the nation of Iraq. *Syriana* shows the recent results of these ongoing inter-national petro-power-plays, and *The Smartest Guys in the Room* unfolds the Enron energy debacle. Other documentaries include: *Roger and Me, Fahrenheit 911, Who Killed the Electric Car?,* and *An Inconvenient Truth.*

Books chronicling the heavy hand of unchecked corporate power are *1984, Brave New World, Atlas Shrugged,* Kim Stanley Robinson's *Mars Trilogy,* and Neal Stephenson's brilliant cyber-novel, *Snow Crash. Confessions of an Economic Hitman* by John Perkins details the devious machinations of current government policy and cor-porate profits at the expense of other countries. Also read *When Corporations Rule the World* by David C. Korten.

C. IN YOUR CREATIONS

Inner Drives Center of Motivation - Lower Solar Plexus: power over money, & Ajna: powerfully focused intelligence dropped to lower motivations.

Show how when the humongous artificial human takes over, it gives (temporary) cover and sanction to real humans' darker impulses: white-collar crimes by CEOs, Congresspersons, and lobbyists.

Trace how some international banks launder money for illegal drugs, guns, nuclear weapons, smuggling, and terrorism; BCCI was a huge scandal in the early 1990s; other big banks have been suspected of same.

Show how the corporation eats its own young; we love to see the bad guy devoured by his own devices.

What if low-paid workers upset over exorbitant CEO pay took hints from the French Revolution?

Big business is notorious for buying out the little guys and shelving their innovations or persecuting the competition to extinction. There's a ready-made underdog hero for you.

Investigate mercenaries working for corporations in hot spots around the world.

There's excellent story fodder in the protests, rebellions, and boycotts in populist Latin America over trade that's really free, not strictly controlled by industrialized nations.

Explore the influence corporations have on academia and science via research grants and built-in censorship.

SECRET SOCIETIES AND SHADOW GOVERNMENTS

Skull and Bones, the Illuminati, Tri-Lateral Commission, Articles of Zion, the Masons, cabals, and cartels? What's real, what's imagined, and what does it matter? Beginning with our early games of hide-and-seek and I've-got-a-secret, humans relish the challenge of the hidden. Grown-up versions of this tendency create secret societies, spies, and conspiracy theories about them.

The basic principle behind secrecy is that it concentrates energy, as a lid on a pot boils water faster. Seclusion also maintains the purity and integrity of a thing, be it a cherry pie, a love affair, or a heinous plot.

Espionage has always been an element of most organizations: everybody wants to know what's going on, to defend themselves, and to expand. Some are willing to do whatever it takes to accomplish that.

The Mystery Schools of Egypt, Tibet, India, Greece, Persia, and mystic Judaism, Christianity, and Islam are initiatory systems to preserve and pass on Ageless Wisdom Teachings. The secrecy was to protect them from the corrupting influence of formal religions and misuse by people with selfish motives. They're all much less secret today, both on purpose — to affect faster positive change in humanity — and also because of increased transparency afforded by the Internet.

However, just as Darth Vader trained with the Jedis, so too we're told the Dark Brotherhood also trains in the Mystery Schools. Without checks and balances, that concentrated hidden power can become heady and addicting and can go really bad when group-think presumes infallibility and invulnerability.

A. In action

The Trilateral Commission and the Carlisle Group, both often accused of controlling world affairs to their benefit, are legitimate organizations, often suspect as to fairness in world trade, banking, and developing countries.

The Masons are a worldwide group of men and women dedicated to the betterment of themselves and mankind, operating under a ritual secrecy but mostly quite open to revealing their principles and sharing information.

Just as the awesome Wizard of Oz was actually a wizened little man behind a curtain, when regents take power too young or are too weak, their viziers or advisors are the real power. The history of royalty teems with stories about shadow governing behind glittering thrones.

During the Cold War, both the U.S. and the U.S.S.R. propped up dictators in client states to hold each other at bay. The CIA and the KGB worked behind the scenes, moving players like chess pieces for secret government agendas.

Corporate interests influencing public policy via lobbyists is a kind of secret government, particularly when it turns to war profiteering via a military-industrial complex. This is an ancient story, but still a rich mine for dramatic conflict.

B. IN MEDIA

Men in Black, X-Files, True Lies, Three Days of the Condor, the Da Vinci Code, Conspiracy Theory, Eyes Wide Shut, National Treasure, Smilla's Sense of Snow. The League of Assassins plagues Batman. *Harry Potter's* Hogwarts is a kind of secret society.

The Morning of the Magicians book by Pauwels and Bergier is packed with various conspiracy theories, from Hitler's advisors studying black magic in Tibet, to the Sumerian god Enki as an emissary from Mars. The superb *Snow Crash* novel combines Sumerian phonemes, cyber-punk, and secret societies.

C. IN YOUR CREATIONS

Inner Drives Center of Motivation - Lower Solar Plexus: separatist ego, suspicion, and paranoia.

Show how holding a secret swells a person up with self importance.

Infiltrating a secret society is always an interesting and usually dangerous challenge.

Give us layers within layers: use metaphors, allegories, and symbols in the rituals to give more in-depth meaning to the action of your story.

Secret societies always have some initiatory process whereby the new member has to prove herself worthy. Those challenges can be part of your character arc.

Industrial espionage is a huge problem for businesses, but seldom seems glamorous. "Aha! We've liberated the formula for the new soda flavor. The world will never be the same," just doesn't have the same ring as saving the country or a way of life. Make techno-spying exciting by focusing on the people who base their existence and worth on business success.

BIG BROTHERS AND BUREAUCRACIES

The paradox of the Big Brother situation is that what we desire — to be protected by a loving big brother can quickly become what we loathe — bullying and suppression as the machine takes over and starts to run the people.

Bureaucrats with job security often run the systems and the so-called leaders are just figureheads (or airheads).

Communism, Socialism, Marxism... all holding some good ideals at their core, turned out to be ponderous and deadly in action. The few countries still operating under these Big Brother bureaucracies are isolationist dictatorships (Burma and North Korea). Maoist insurgencies still smolder in Latin America and some small Asian countries.

Big Brother typically suppresses and controls information, typically through censorship, co-opting media, or outright killing of journalists and intellectuals.

This clenched-jaw *deva* of total control combines parsimonious Dweller stuff, Dark Force inertia, and, it sometimes seems, the full weight of Darth Vader with an MBA from Hell U.

A. IN ACTION

Ancient writing reveals that people griped about governments and bureaucracies as far back as dynastic Egypt. The Catholic Church took over the bureaucracy of the fallen Roman Empire and acquired a cumbersome system that still stymies progress and self correction.

Prohibition in '20s–'30s America. Our 1950s black list with Senator Joe McCarthy and Roy Cohn. George W. Bush's inefficient and ineffective Homeland Security agency, unwarranted surveillance, rollbacks of *habeas corpus*, and extensions of government power at the expense of civil rights.

Less deadly but still quite frustrating are the bureaucracies of everyday existence: the DMV, the phone company, insurance, banks.

B. IN MEDIA

1984, Brave New World, Brazil, Office Space, The Office TV series, *Guilty by Suspicion, Good Night and Good Luck.* A fun section in *The Hitchhiker's Guide to the Galaxy* movie takes Zaphod Beeblebrox into the maddening maze of Vogon bureaucracy. The last scene in *Raiders of the Lost Ark* descends into bureaucracy when the dangerous Ark is wheeled into a huge warehouse as Indy's assured it's in the hands of "top men."

The Borg from *Star Trek* is/are a perfect example of exquisite organization gone really, really wrong.

German writer Franz Kafka's stories epitomized the horror inherent in mindless organizations. Situations of random unfathomable obstacles and oppression are called Kafkaesque. Orson Welles made a movie from Kafka's paranoid novel *The Trial.*

Dilbert cartoons.

C. IN YOUR CREATIONS

Inner Drives Center of Motivation – Throat: drive to organize and oversee, & Lower Solar Plexus: drive to control others.

Show the tipping point when the organization gets so big it gets impersonal. Systems theory usually puts that at one hundred people. See the effect on particular individuals who still try to operate the old way.

Show how a person with rigid tendencies who is afraid of freedom finds bureaucracy comfortable. Then toss them into free fall and watch the fireworks.

Investigate what it takes to dissolve or destroy a Big Brother system. Why did the Soviet Union implode? Why is Chinese Communism eroding?

Show how freedom of information effects Big Brother.

Have your heroine find the weak spot in a bureaucracy and exploit it.

Privatize a bureaucracy. Show the positive, such as commercial space flight; or negative, such as the failed California energy grid under Enron.

Offer clever ways to navigate bureaucracies, serious or funny.

EVIL EMPIRES

For all the reasons in this chapter, giant empires can and most often do go bad. They may start out as sheer adventurism or a search for resources, but once you've taken new land, you have to hold it. That requires resources and management, then that requires growth, so you need to expand further, then the expansion requires resources and management, etc. Staying in power and growing often demands the violent suppression of opposition, as well as forming alliances with unsavory people.

The Catholic Church took over the structure and reach of the Roman Empire in the 4th century; some have called their reign evil... it's certainly been a heavy hand. The British also claimed to be descendents of the Romans via a convenient myth, and in the way their Empire emulated Rome's vast reach. The Pax Romana (Roman peace) and Pax Britannica of those vast empires were bought by sword and bloodshed, but they did open routes for trade, culture, and people to flow more freely. Evil, or just breaking eggs to make omelets?

A. IN ACTION

Oh, just read the history books and watch The History Channel.

World War II and the Cold War both pitted Evil Empires intent upon world domination against other nations fighting for world freedom. Many of today's conflicts are leftover Cold War proxy-wars, particularly in Africa and Afghanistan.

It was President Ronald Regan who called the Soviets the Evil Empire and it was the U.S. that trained and armed the Taliban to fight them. "The enemy of my enemy is my friend." Yeah, maybe... until that enemy goes away and then your new friends may become your new enemies.

B. IN MEDIA

Will and Ariel Durant's multivolume *The Story of Civilization* reads like an epic novel and will give you many story ideas. Edward Gibbon's *The Decline and Fall of the Roman Empire* is also a vivid classic, often quoted in warning about America.

Little Big Man, The Last of the Mohicans, and *The Mission* are about Europeans colonizing the so-called New World, though the Amerindians had been there tens of thousands of years and had empires to rival the Egyptians.

The *Star Wars* movies pit the Evil Empire against the valiant rebels, with Darth Vader and the wicked Sith Lords determined to wipe out all opposition. They didn't figure on Luke Skywalker, Han Solo, and Princess Leia.

The BBC TV series *The Jewel in the Crown* examines darker sides of the British Empire in India during World War II. The HBO series *Rome* and the BBC series *I, Claudius* reveal bloody rottenness at the heart of the Roman Empire.

The Lord of the Rings trilogy pits the good Fellowship of the Rings folk against the evil empire of dark Sauron and his deadly creatures.

Pitch Black and *The Chronicles of Riddick* have one guy (Vin Diesel) fighting the entire empire of half-dead Necromongers.

C. IN YOUR CREATIONS

Inner Drives Center of Motivation – Ajna, dropped: empires can't begin without incredible intellect, courage, and strength. Once that focus drops to sheer power-mongering, greed, and sensual indulgence, the end is not far away.

There's a rich spectrum of plot and character examples from history. Select the little-known stories or people and expand on those unique perspectives.

Show how some Nazis believed they were helping bring about the evolution of humanity by culling the race of undesirables. No doubt some conquistadors thought it was better for native Americans to lose their lives but save their souls. How did those people deal with what they had to do to accomplish their "higher" goals: glee, anguish, guilt, indifference? What parallels can you show in modern radical Islam? Fundamentalist Christianity?

Many stories already tell the ancient Briton's side of the Roman conquest. So, let's see more about the Amerindians conquered by Spanish conquistadors, or the people who remained in Babylon after the Mongols conquered it in 1215.

If you found hidden books by the Incas or Aztecs, what might you learn about those powerful, rather bloody empires?

Use the shifting-scope story device to show how a big Empire affects one little person; or vise versa.

What if the Empire got reformed? Would utopia be so boring someone would just have to rebel?

WAR! HUH, WHAT IS IT GOOD FOR?

Though there can be great virtue and value in the Warrior Path, there's also a really Dark Side to it.

Groupthink is essential if you want to get a good war going. No individual in their right mind would take up arms and go into harm's way with a good chance of killing and being killed unless there were a seemingly good reason for it. Granted some people are prone to violence, but they usually prefer to inflict it, not receive it. Going to war implies both.

Patriotic jingoism, stirring speeches, and a whipped-up climate of aggression or defense can fling otherwise sensible individuals into a groupthink frenzy. Whether it's Popes offering salvation to soldiers on Crusade to retake the Holy Land, Hitler's call for *lebensraum* (living room — room to expand) and speedy evolution to *ubermensch* (superman) destiny, radical Islam's urge to purge the world of the Great Satan Western culture, the power and allure of many like minds can suck you in like a whirlpool.

A. IN ACTION

Talk to anyone who's ever been to boot camp, where individualism is pressed out and groupthink is shoved in.

Soldiers going AWOL are often breaking out of groupthink.

From Thucydides' on-the-ground account of the 5th-century BCE Peloponnesian Wars to soldiers' blogs from Afghanistan and Iraq, waging war has always depended on groupthink.

B. IN MEDIA

Watch the opening speech in *Patton*. Leni Riefenstahl's *Triumph of the Will* is so effective it might even inspire you to sign up for the SS (until you stop and think about it). Stanley Kubrick had a wry take on groupthink in *Dr. Strangelove* and a tragic one in *Full Metal Jacket*. *The Thin Red Line* showed individual soldiers switching between groupthink and love musings, ambition mongering, or spiritual contemplation as required by orders and enemy fire. Tom Hanks was a reluctant groupthink leader in *Saving Private Ryan*.

Shakespeare's St. Crispin's Day speech for *Henry V* has been repeated to rousing effect: Kenneth Branagh as Henry urges his British soldiers against the French at Avignon, Bill Pullman as a U.S. President inspires a global group of fighter pilots against the aliens in *Independence Day*, Tom Berringer as President Teddy Roosevelt does it in *Rough Riders*.

Pat Barker's award-winning *Regeneration* novels personalize the tragedies of groupthink for soldiers caught up in the madness of WWI trench warfare. Kubrick's *Paths of Glory* illustrates the perversity behind that madness.

Rudyard Kipling's war poems and stories scathe groupthink, while Tennyson's poem *The Charge of the Light Brigade* ennobles it with "Theirs not to reason why, theirs but to do and die."

Joseph Conrad details a descent into groupthink in his novel *The Heart of Darkness*; writer John Milius and director Francis Ford Coppola give it a war setting in *Apocalypse Now*.

All war stories by definition deal with groupthink.

C. IN YOUR CREATIONS

Inner Drives Center of Motivation - Lower Solar Plexus: separatism and small groups, & Root: survival and death.

Have your leader do a version of the ever-popular, ever-powerful St. Crispin's Day speech, "We few, we happy few, we band of brothers...."

Take a cue from *The Thin Red Line* and show various characters differently enthralled in groupthink, or not.

Delineate the decline as idealism goes bad and groupthink goes dark, ala the IRA and the Palestinian-Israeli conflict.

Show the evolution of warrior groupthink from a small patrol to high command. The *Sharpe's Rifles* series starring Sean Bean follows a lower-class soldier's rise to officer in the Napoleonic wars, with all the problems of shifting his group identity and getting others to recognize that shift.

Enrich your military groupthink with setbacks like Mission Creep (the slam dunk expands into a quagmire), Blowback (reverberations from the battlefield), unintended consequences, etc.

Militaries tend to fight the last war, rather than clearly analyzing the current situation; it's a great opportunity for conflict between your heroine and the groupthinking establishment marching towards disaster.

CONCLUSION

Groupthink in its many versions offers a rich source of ominous villains, dangerous situations, and dramatic conflict. This hive/herd tendency causes huge problems which most of us encounter in some way. Whether your heroine is standing up and directly fighting groupthink or whether a groupthink situation is the background of your story, be sure to show us that it's often a good idea gone bad. Also show us how difficult it is to turn around, stop, or destroy the juggernaut of mindless movement. Just remember, resistance is *not* useless, and the resistance is what makes a good story.

8.
WITCHES, WIZARDS, AND WARLOCKS

✦ Shamans

✦ Witchcraft as science

✦ Wizardry as political science

✦ The Dark Arts

✦ Witch hunts

Harry Potter, The Wizard of Oz, Charmed, Buffy the Vampire Slayer... in the midst of the most scientifically advanced civilizations in history we're seeing a resurgence of interest in magic. Some say it's a reaction to the emotionless impersonality of technology. Some say it's always been there, it's just safer to come out of the broom closet these days.

Our earliest stories feature wicked witches, fairy godmothers, powerful warlocks, and magical wizards. Before we have scientific or sophisticated explanations for the wonders of the world around us, we personify the mystery of our existence in human-like beings of great power, the same way we create gods.

Most often these W's of story are humans with special powers, though occasionally they're exiles or invaders from other realms. All have the ability to work with Nature, combine its aspects into new forms, and bend it with their Will. They can also assess people's foibles and fantasies and use them for assistance, annoyance, or annihilation.

There are so many stories, books, games, Web sites, and organizations offering in-depth information about magic that additional research will be easy for you. Here are some characteristics and categories of these hair-raising individuals whose special talents can twist the nature of reality, aid or threaten your hero, and be fascinating story characters.

CHARACTERISTICS

Hyper-alert. Hyper-analytical. They see patterns where others do not see them and create patterns where they did not exist. They see past the symptom to the root cause. They understand and manipulate the laws of Nature. They understand and manipulate human psychology. Whether showy or secretive, they're always aware of their affect on others. They manipulate others via voice pitch, tone, cadence; hand and body movement to catch and direct attention; substances to alter mind and body.

If nonhuman or superhuman, they may manipulate the very laws of Nature.

SHAMANS

The earliest human societies include someone designated as the liaison to the spirit world. Cave paintings and ancient art reflect an awareness of altered states thought to be induced by drumming, singing, dancing, and the ingestion of various natural hallucinogens. Sometimes pain is part of the process.

Some part of us knows that what we know isn't all there is. The person who can supply answers to the mysteries of life becomes valuable to a group's collective sanity, but can also twist that power for personal gain and the oppression of others. Fear of the unknown is a powerful tool, and when wielded by a shaman or magician with a healthy knowledge of human psychology, can be terrifying.

A. IN ACTION

Most pharmaceutical companies research traditional medicines all around the world, as in *Medicine Man,* starring Sean Connery.

In modern-day sub-Saharan Africa, traditional medicine (*muti*) is still practiced by many. Though quite often helpful, some *muti* involves mutilation and murder. Human body parts are thought to contain lots of power, made more potent by the victim's screams. Scotland Yard believes recent murders among African immigrants in England might be *muti* killings.

B. IN MEDIA

The No. 1 Ladies Detective Agency series of novels by Alexander McCall Smith contains references to *muti*.

In *The Emerald Forest* film an American boy is kidnapped and raised by an Amazonian tribe. Coached by the shaman, he learns to navigate the spirit world.

The award-winning Canadian docu-drama *The Journals of Knud Rasmussen* shows what happens to an Inuit shaman when Christianity and modernity encroach on the old ways.

C. IN YOUR CREATIONS

Inner Drives Centers of Motivation – Root: sheer survival, & Throat Center: clever observation and manipulation of nature and human nature.

Show how the Wizard/Witch came to be set apart: red hair, albino, disabled, exceptionally ugly or beautiful, homosexual, smarter or dumber than most....

Another typical way shamans (as well as creative people) awaken to their powers is a period of illness or isolation, usually when young. Pain, fear, or great desire can also trigger the appearance of the magic.

As with anything supernatural, you can have the villain not believe in it and use others' fears to manipulate them; or have the villain believe in it but be corrupted to the Dark Side.

A treat for your audience is to have the villain not believe, but then it turns out the magic actually does work, and they're defeated by their own conjuring.

As science discovers more about how the body and mind work, we learn that many magical cures make perfect scientific sense. Stories that bring rational thinking to former superstitions can offer surprises to satisfy both believers and skeptics.

WITCHCRAFT AS SCIENCE

The Wisdom Teachings are astute observations about nature and humans made over eons of time, passed down in formulas, theories, practices, and stories. Being able to predict the movements of the sun, moon, and stars is beyond most, even today. Yet archaeology reveals that many ancient cultures had highly developed scientists who had the orbit of Venus and the precession of the equinoxes down perfect, and they built huge monuments to prove it.

Witches are traditionally wise women who can heal people. And curse them. Wizards supposedly read the past and foresee the future. Both are assumed to be able to influence the present and shape the future.

A. IN ACTION

Before it was common knowledge, anyone who could get their hands on the Chinese invention gunpowder or the still-mysterious Greek fire (a floating, flammable liquid you can't put out with water) would be considered a sorcerer. Those who favor ancient astronaut theories note how many myths refer to "fire from the skies" and the similarity to air strikes, napalm, and nukes. Is it ancient wizardry or ancient science?

B. IN MEDIA

Wizards Merlin, Morgaine, and Taliesin wield magic-science in the Arthurian stories. Author Norma Lorre Goodrich has a comprehensive book series that offers fiction writers rich information.

The *Conan* series of books and movies features lots of sorcery, some based on science, some on sheer magic. Usually wizards are the bad guys and only Conan's sword and physical strength save the day with sheer brawn over brains. *Xena: Warrior Princess* combines both brawn and brains to battle sorcery in the 1990s TV series.

Techno-Mages in the TV series *Babylon 5* and *Crusade* cloak their advanced science in magic to better impress the uninformed, as with hologram projections.

C. IN YOUR CREATIONS

Inner Drives Center of Motivation – Ajna Center: the conscious combination of other Centers and abilities, the manipulation of time.

Arthur C. Clarke famously observed that any sufficiently advanced technology is indistinguishable from magic. Show us how one person's technology is another person's magic.

Show us the learning process: thrill of discovery, first missteps, fine-tuning, and results of success. Recall Sorcerer's Apprentice Mickey Mouse in *Fantasia,* who used a spell to get brooms carrying water buckets but didn't know the spell to make them stop flooding the workshop.

Star Wars' Luke Skywalker and the Jedi Knights' training sessions teach the physics of metaphysics combined with personal strength and stamina. Research martial arts training and take it to the next level for your characters.

WIZARDRY AS POLITICAL SCIENCE

Using mystery, aspiration, and fear, a priestly class can manipulate the emotions of a populace. Using chants, dance, incense, and architecture, priestly wizardry guides people to desired actions. Kind of like how political machines and consumer marketing use media today.

While spirituality includes transformation of self, most religions are about everyday behavior here on earth, with promise of pleasure or pain beyond. As teaching tools for social propriety and control mechanisms for an otherwise restless populace, religions are very effective. Religion is also very dangerous for the same reasons. See more at radical fundamentalism.

A. IN ACTION

Some African priestesses still symbolically cut up warriors and toss them in a bubbling cauldron, then seemingly pull them out whole, supposedly invincible and ready for battle against modern weapons.

The family of Russian Czar Nicolas was controlled by Rasputin, a charismatic, corrupt priest who supposedly healed their hemophiliac son with his magic powers. He also seduced noblewomen and dabbled in politics to the extent that Russian nobles (probably assisted by British Secret Service) assassinated him in 1916, though legend has it they had to try many times and he's really not dead (just living on that same island with Elvis, JFK, Jimi Hendrix, and Janis Joplin).

John Dee was a brilliant 16th-century British mathematician and occultist, advisor to Queen Elizabeth I. This accomplished scientist and alchemist is a featured character in many stories, including Umberto Eco's *Foucault's Pendulum*, a smart and humorous novel about magic and conspiracies.

B. IN MEDIA

In the Bible, Israelite leader Joshua made the sun and the moon stand still. Scholars differ on whether that was just bragging or a reference to some astronomical event.

Frank Herbert's *Dune* novels feature the Bene Gesserit, wise women who manipulate empires using seduction, illusion, and the occasional assassination.

The Lord of the Rings books and movies find the politics and statecraft of humans, hobbits, elves, and dwarves intricately bound up by the sorcery of the rings. Sauron, Saruman, and Gandalf all use wizardry for political ends.

Wicked: The Life and Times of the Wicked Witch of the West imagines the ugly green witch from *The Wizard of Oz* as a sensitive ethical girl, determined to help overthrow an oppressive regime, frustrated by her friend Glinda the Good's ditzy naiveté.

C. IN YOUR CREATIONS

Inner Drives Centers of Motivation – Ajna: site for magic, & Lower Solar Plexus: political manipulations, personal power over others.

These W's should be smart, science-savvy, and politically astute.

Show how W's assess a group's common beliefs (political, religious, economic) and then manipulate them.

Reveal the manipulated group's lack of a certain knowledge (eclipses, sulfur, penicillin) and how that makes them vulnerable.

Imagine the perfect propaganda illusion for your heroine's agenda, be it a fearsome enemy or a fabulous treasure.

The change from someone who knows information to someone who misuses it is a fascinating process. Show us the decline and fall of such a person.

THE DARK ARTS

At Harry Potter's Hogwarts school you study Defenses Against the Dark Arts. So, where do you study the Dark Arts themselves? Same place you study the Light Arts. The tools are the same; it's the motive that makes the difference.

Just as Darth Vader and Obi Wan Kenobi of *Star Wars* both went through Jedi Knight training, so too do the Dark Wizards and Witches go through the same training as Wise Men and Women — up to a point. *That point is vital for your storytelling.* It is where self-sacrifice is called for. Those who go down the Left Hand Path to the Dark Brotherhood are unwilling to give of themselves for others. Those in the White Brotherhood live to serve the One Life, even at the cost of their own.

Ancient traditions and New Age speculations place secret wizard schools high in the Himalayas, the Andes, and Mount Shasta as well as underground in Egypt, Antarctica, and Phoenix, Arizona. Hindus, Egyptians, Jewish Cabalists, Muslim Sufis, Celtic Druids, medieval alchemists, pagans, and Wiccans all teach the ways of nature, human nature, and how to manipulate both.

Though it can produce conflict or comedy, corruption at the lower levels of the Dark Arts is obviously not as dangerous as with those who've gained access to the deeper secrets of nature and conscious creativity — think young Lucius Malfoy in *Harry Potter* versus Saruman the dark wizard in *The Lord of the Rings*. Oriental lore tells of entire societies of religious monks and nuns who went bad and stayed that way, using their mystical skills and martial arts to play heck with rival monasteries and unwary innocents.

Some legends say the suprahuman entities who rule cultures, civilizations, and continents can be corrupted, and the loss of Lemuria and Atlantis, as well as the downfall of some empires, might be due to these Great Ones going over to the Dark Brotherhood.

A. IN ACTION

In the Bible and other quasi-historical accounts, human wielders of the Dark Arts are often responsible for the rise and fall of kingdoms and cultures.

Alchemy is the study of natural laws, philosophy, and esoterics that has flourished deep within all religions for two-and-a-half millennia in Europe, India, and the Near and Middle East. Isaac Newton was an alchemist, and alchemy is considered the crucible of modern chemistry. Alchemy encourages positive spiritual transformation, but some alchemists do turn to the Dark Side.

Eastern occultism flourished alongside Einstein's new science at the turn of the last century, spawning many magical Western societies such as the Golden Dawn. Modern paganism and many New Age systems grew out of these early groups. Members sometimes turn Dark, and charlatans still cheat gullible people.

Self-proclaimed wizard and Golden Dawn leader Aleister Crowley was famous for his fondness for Dark Arts, particularly sex magic. Esoteric lore notes that a burst of light is released into the astral world at the moment of orgasm or violent death. Many magical traditions use sex and death in their rituals to draw the attention of entities from other realms and to pay them off for their assistance in this realm. It's the same principle involved in religious sacrifice, be it human, animal or in milder versions, flowers or finances.

B. IN MEDIA

Many fiction and nonfiction books have been written about Nazism and the Occult, some of them pretty darn spooky.

Stanley Kubrick's film *Eyes Wide Shut* features ritual sex magic. *The Mummy* movies villain is still around because of powerful anti-death magic.

Crouching Tiger, Hidden Dragon introduced movie viewers worldwide to the exhilarating genre mix of Eastern Dark Arts with high-flying martial arts. Plot drivers in the Japanese anime film *Spirited Away* are the Dark Arts.

The TV series *Charmed* and *Buffy the Vampire Slayer* are full of the Dark Arts used by young people juggling the senior prom with saving the world from evil sorcerers, demons, and vampires.

Anne Rice's book *The Queen of the Damned* reaches back into the sands of time to the Egyptian source of the vampiric Dark Art.

His Dark Materials books and *The Golden Compass* movie are fabulous explorations of the consequences of both humans and gods using the Dark Arts.

C. IN YOUR CREATIONS

Inner Drives Center of Motivation – Lower Solar Plexus: the power grab, & Ajna: magic central.

What tools can your characters use to bewitch others? Try sex, fear, money, power, ambition, religious devotion, and even spiritual aspiration.

Most temptations of major holy men and women include really big stuff such as world domination. Be sure in your stories the temptations and rewards fit the environment, and that you set up your character's desires early on.

The Dark Arts go waaaaaaaay back in time, so show that with old books, references, ancient artifacts, creaky advisors.

The Dark Arts are a perversion of the physics of metaphysics, which is mostly just science that doesn't have instruments to measure it yet. Pitting your wizard against a scientist who figures out how it works could send sparks flying.

WITCH HUNTS

Most witchcraft is simply the alignment of human will with Nature's ways, usually to beneficial results. Problems arise when those who aren't as aware feel supernatural forces are involved. Because humans are often spooked by what they don't understand, the supposed powers of the W's seem scary, and as we've seen above, some Dark W's do take advantage with their superior skills.

Humans also typically shoot down those who rise above the norm. Accusations of witchcraft and wizardry have an astonishing coincidence with rivalry and revenge. Be it the witch burnings of centuries past, the Red Scare trials of the 1950s, or continuing persecution in many cultures today, the "witch" label can unfortunately condemn people to exile, loss of property and profession, torture, and even death.

A. IN ACTION

Masons and Jews are often accused of witchcraft and persecuted for being different and exclusive. Blood sacrifices and "unholy kisses" are often included in the accusations.

The Yale University secret society Skull and Bones, with many political leader alumni, is rumored by conspiracy theorists to include wizardly secrets and sex-death rituals.

In Ghana and many other places in Africa today, women who are too successful, too old, or simply in the way are often accused of witchcraft and sent off to exile in wretched witch camps.

B. IN MEDIA

In the Bible, Moses pits his magic against Pharaoh's wizards as they turn staffs into snakes and rivers into blood.

The Salem witch trials are the subject for many books and media, as are the four centuries of witch hunts throughout Europe during the Catholic Church's Inquisition.

The gorgeous film *Dangerous Beauty*, based on real-life courtesan Veronica Franco, finds her accused of witchcraft when 16th-century Venice is hit by the plague.

Monty Python has an hilarious skit about no one expecting the Spanish Inquisition.

Wizards at war is a huge subplot in *The Lord of the Rings*.

There's the entire game genre of Sword and Sorcery, such as *Dungeons and Dragons*.

C. IN YOUR CREATIONS

Inner Drives Center of Motivation – Ajna: that magic center (for the accused), & Sacral: the fear-sex-money center (for the accusers).

In stories about this situation you'll want three factions: the accused, the accusers, and the manipulated populace.

Witch hunts usually spring out of strict religious-superstitious societies, or societies under stress. Show the build up of societal problems and that there are few other ways for people to express their fears and hostilities.

Show some of the actions of the accused in ways that could indeed be misinterpreted: they alone reap a bountiful harvest because they alone planted at the correct moon phase; they take a gift to a new baby and the baby gets sick; they're attractive and others' spouses eyes wander, etc.

Politics plays a huge role in witch hunts. Show the scare tactics used to intimidate and paralyze the populace, then how the controllers turn their targets into scapegoats.

CONCLUSION

We've looked at some aspects of how these characters fit into a society, a situation, a story. Crafting them as more than cardboard bad guys can greatly enrich your creations. Keep in mind the Dark Side Witches, Wizards, and Warlocks will be prideful. After all, they know more than most people and can seemingly control the environment in many dimensions. That makes them dangerous, including to themselves.

Though black magic and dark wizards are usually ominous, you can use this archetype in comedy, too, like the comedy-romance *Witches of Eastwick* starring Jack Nicholson or the classic musical *Damn Yankees!* Most of Stephen King's stories include ill-doing magical people, creatures, or machines, and the ancient world of fairy tales is filled with these types.

Giving characters varying degrees of magical abilities, from basic intuition to full galactic dominance, allows you to mix and match them for dramatic conflict, like the wizards Saruman (bad) and Gandalf (good) in *LOTR*. Also use a sliding scale along which they can grow or decline, like Willow the teen witch learning to control her addiction to magic in *Buffy*.

Using magic in your stories allows us to glimpse the mysteries of life and experience the wonders of unseen worlds.

9.
GHOSTS, GHOULS, AND GHASTLY GODS

+ **Ye gods**

+ **Nature spirits**

+ **Ghosts**

+ **Vampires, werewolves, zombies**

+ **Monsters**

+ **Aliens**

+ **Haunted things and places**

It starts with the monster in the closet, moves on to the ghost stories around the fire, and graduates to a fascination with unexplained phenomena. The eternal popularity of scary stories is evidence that most of us love to be mystified and sometimes a little terrified, maybe because it reminds us that we're alive, maybe just for the adrenaline rush.

Humans demand meaning and always come up with explanations for any experience, whether created by external or internal stimuli. Since we tend to create pictures with our imaginations and anthropomorphize the world around us, it's no wonder we turn our sometimes vague perceptions into ghosts and ghouls, angels and aliens.

On the other hand, some myth systems offer taxonomies of non-human entities with hierarchies, job descriptions, and genealogies so extensive you think there must be something to it. Anyone who's ever sensed other presences, "heard voices," or "seen" shades of dead people knows that the perceptions themselves are quite real, and debates have raged for millennia over the nature of reality, so who can really say for certain?

Science can point to which part of the brain lights up under specific stimuli, but we're not quite sure why some people seem to perceive from afar, or why you sometimes know who's phoning, even without Caller ID. Esoterics posits we have an "etheric body" that is larger and more sensitive to the nonphysical realm than is our physical form.

The Mystery Schools teach that the astral (emotional) plane is where many of these entities exist and that any human can access that plane on purpose through drugs, dance, drink, ritual, sensory deprivation, special training, or through illness or accident.

Archetypes and *devas* created on the astral plane are sustained by emotions, so just like in lots of sci-fi stories where a creature feeds off intense emotion, these *devas* get stronger with attention and celebrity. There's a speech in *Wes Craven's New Nightmare* about how story character Freddie Krueger became an embodiment of evil who's now crossing over from the astral to the physical plane.

There are many books, Web sites, training systems, people, and media dedicated to all this lore, so deeper research on these topics will be easy for you.

YE GODS

Bad gods play a part in most religions. Typically they're the old gods who got whupped by the new gods, or they're the other guy's gods.

CHARACTERISTICS

Pick a type from the "Bad Boys and Girls" chapter and just give them lots more power.

A. IN ACTION

The Bible's Yahweh was very strict about "no other gods," and when Mohammed took over the Kaaba in Mecca, he first destroyed the 360 idols that'd been worshipped there for centuries.

The Goddess movement posits a nomadic warlike male god system overthrowing a peaceful female system and setting up a patriarchy. Though some art, archaeology, and mythology support some of that idea, debates rage over interpretation of the data.

B. IN MEDIA

Ancient Hindu scriptures, Greek myths, and many other mythologies tell of war between one group of gods and another. Harry Hamlin as Perseus witnesses this in *Clash of the Titans*.

Maria Gymbutas, Rhian Eisler, and many others write about the displaced goddess. *The Harlot by the Side of the Road* reveals Biblical evidence for Israelite persecution of goddess religions. *The Mists of Avalon* pits patriarchal Christianity against the goddess ways of Arthurian Briton. *The Da Vinci Code* does the Mary Magdalene version of the displaced goddess theory.

C. IN YOUR CREATIONS

Inner Drives Centers of Motivation – Crown: the door to higher realms, & all others: as most deities tend to act like humans.

Since deities are usually created in the image of humans, have the gods reflect your story's conflicts at a greater level of reach and consequence.

Remote deities aren't very interesting; get yours in actual touch with individual humans.

If humans are pitting their deities against each other, as in religious wars, what do the deities think? Are they amused? Annoyed? Apathetic? Appalled?

Show us how deities get their power, and how it can be lost.

NATURE SPIRITS

Since humans came so late to the party, most mythologies cite creatures who ruled the world before us, some of whom aren't too thrilled we're here.

You doubt there's more to reality than our human senses can perceive? Just watch a cat stalking "invisible" things. Paleobiology discovered that early mammals had four color-sensitive cones in their eyes rather than today's three. Back then, nocturnal mammals could see infrared just like insects and birds still do. What if people who see auras have some kind of throwback vision thing and are seeing in the infrared spectrum?

CHARACTERISTICS

Not bound by the laws of nature or DNA. Species can mix with kingdoms: mermaids, tree maidens, fire monsters. Carry a grudge against humans. Seriously lacking some human aspect: can't love (or sometimes can't have sex), can't eat, bound to a certain place. Vulnerable to certain things (iron is kryptonite for some).

A. IN ACTION

Goblins, trolls, fairies, sprites, demons... these nonhuman beings populate folk tales, legends, and myths. Some see them as projections of human fears or desires, some as personifications of elemental forces and things, some see them as faint remnants of past eras, others as trespassers from other dimensions.

Responsible teachers warn students not to get caught up in the astral phenomenon that's a by-product of some meditation and yoga techniques. An activation of the Solar Plexus chakra is said to give greater access to the astral planes where people frequently see angels and aliens and develop ESP powers. It's one of the crossroads that can lead to the Dark Side, lured by the seeming power of controlling elementals, fairies, and such. It will only come to tears — and to good scary stories.

B. IN MEDIA

Arab legends feature evil djinn, or genies. European folk tales warn hikers away from fairy rings and to watch out for trolls under bridges.

Offering both science and mystery, the villains in the film *Photographing Fairies* are deadly fairies. Tinkerbell in *Peter Pan* is so jealous she tries to kill Wendy.

The *Harry Potter* series has gremlins, goblins, bad fairies, and more. *The Lord of the Rings* trilogy has a wealth of elves, fairies, trolls, dwarves, orcs, etc.

C. IN YOUR CREATIONS

Inner Drives Centers of Motivation – Solar Plexus (both Lower and Aspirational): supernatural perceptions and phenomena.

How would earth-based elementals such as trolls or dwarves react to their modern cousin — silicon chips? Would they free them from the mainframe prisons or commune directly with them, no keyboards required?

Know what your demons and sprites want: to be left alone, to get rid of humans, vengeance, to rule, to eat, to sleep, to finally die?

Ideally, humans are supposed to help these creatures evolve in consciousness, as they help us interact with the physical world. How could your story's humans partner up with the elementals to solve global warming, construction costs (moving giant stones as in legends), transportation, etc.?

GHOSTS AND POLTERGEISTS

Unlike the creatures in the last category who exist in and of themselves, ghosts are the leftovers of creatures, usually humans. They're most commonly thought of as stranded souls of dead humans either unaware they're dead or really pissed off about it and determined to wreak some havoc.

Exorcists know that these phenomena often result from a suppressed Sacral chakra, particularly in hormonal pubescent youth, as all that emotional energy surges through the poor kid looking for somewhere to go. Without proper creative outlets, drawers open, knives fly about, and tables toddle across rooms while terrified teens shriek in horror. Or so the theory goes.

CHARACTERISTICS

Usually one strong emotion motivates ghosts' actions: anger, sadness, vengeance, loneliness, regret, etc. Their presence lowers the temperature. They usually appear as they did in their last alive moment. Animals can often perceive them.

A. IN ACTION

Many people think they've encountered a ghost. Common beliefs are that ghosts are not bound by laws of nature (walk through walls, fly, invisible). Ghosts have a limited affect on the physical world (often can't speak, can't move things). Poltergeists can move physical objects.

Ghostbusting and exorcisms use magic, chants, religious rites, herbs, and spiritual intervention to either get the ghost to vacate a place, or to help them move on to the afterworld.

B. IN MEDIA

All the spooky ghost stories, books, movies, and TV series.

Ghost Busters, Poltergeist, Beetlejuice, X-Files, and many more. In *Ghost,* dead guy Patrick Swayze can't leave until he solves the mystery of his own death and protects his beloved wife.

In the anime film *Spirited Away* young human Chihiro enters a world of trapped, disembodied spirits and helps release some of them.

The Sixth Sense is from the point of view of the ghost, Bruce Willis, who helps the human boy figure out how to help other ghosts resolve their issues and move on.

C. IN YOUR CREATIONS

Inner Drives Centers of Motivation – Lower Solar Plexus: where most souls exit the physical body, and what ties those souls to earthly life.

From the "What Dark Side?" chapter, determine what your ghost believes about the afterlife, evil, etc. so you can keep their motives and actions internally consistent.

Pit two characters with different belief systems against each other. What if your ghost does not believe in ghosts?

Explore various cultures' annual festivals for ghosts to get ideas for plots and characters: the Mexican Day of the Dead, the Chinese Festival of Hungry Ghosts, Celtic All Hallow's Eve, etc.

Do animals have ghosts? Do buildings? Cities? If so, what would they do? What would they want? How could you "bust" them, or send them to their next step?

VAMPIRES, WEREWOLVES, ZOMBIES, AND OTHER EX-HUMANS

Whether they're just symbols of psychological traits gone bad or the remnants of ancient genetic engineering, these creatures have filled our stories forever. Most cultures have local versions of these things: in Southeast Asia it's were-tigers, in South America it's were-jaguars. Likewise there are local explanations of how they came to be and how to kill them.

CHARACTERISTICS

Some remnants of their humanity remain — sometimes physical, sometimes psychological. Often have super-strength. Often seemingly human except on full moons, at night, when blood-hungry, etc. Often can only be killed by certain things: sunlight, silver bullets, magic earth, etc.

A. IN ACTION

Though many people claim to have encountered (or to actually be) these creatures, there's no scientifically accepted real-world evidence. That's good news for storytellers – let your imagination run wild.

According to most anthropological studies, zombies seem to be humans hypnotized through ritual and drugs, not enlivened dead bodies as voodoo practitioners would have you believe.

B. IN MEDIA

The horror genre is huge, and many hinge on these weird creatures.

In some of the classic *Dr. Jekyll and Mr. Hyde* films, he turns werewolfish in his Mr. Hyde side. *An American Werewolf in London* is a cult movie from the '80s, and from the same era, the *Howling* movies.

For psychologically complex vampires and demons, and a lot of good fun, watch the TV series *Buffy the Vampire Slayer*. Ann Rice's *Vampire Chronicles* book series offers an ancient explanation of how all that blood sucking got started, back in ancient Egypt in a bid for immortality. *The Hunger*, starring Susan Sarandon and David Bowie, is a classy and poignant version; you must read Bram Stoker's *Dracula*, the modern daddy of vampire stories.

Cult favorite *Night of the Living Dead* is a classic zombie movie where the dead try to eat the living. In the comedy *Death Becomes Her* Goldie Hawn and Meryl Streep are glamorous zombies, rivals for beauty and attention.

C. IN YOUR CREATIONS

Inner Drives Centers of Motivation – Root: death, survival.

Experiment with other human-animal mixtures.

Besides blood, what would vampires want? One story has them going for pituitary glands to stay young. Play with the principle of ritual cannibalism — you eat what you want to become: heart = courageous, brain = clever, genitals = potent.

These afflictions hint at addictions; have their human cravings directly correspond to their animal actions. Or play against it and have each side loathe what their other self does: the wolf can't stand cigarette smoke, the vampire faints at the sight of blood, the human is a city girl, or she is allergic to dogs, etc.

MONSTERS

Our first bouts with monsters are usually the ones under our beds and in our closets. As we grow up, our monsters become more sophisticated. Fear of the unknown is the cause, incredible creatures are the result.

CHARACTERISTICS

Nonhuman, so pretty much anything goes. To be actual antagonists there must be some slight ability to relate to humans: as food, as toys, as punching bags, as obstacles to their goals, as slaves, as mates.

Captain Taggart (Tim Allen) snaps in *Galaxy Quest* when counseled by a fellow actor Alan Rickman to determine the motivation of the monster chasing him, "It's a rock monster — it doesn't have any motivation!"

A. IN ACTION

Like much of art, monsters are an exaggeration of reality. Sea monsters are real storms personified or symbolically stand for emotions run amok. Some think dragons are a genetic memory of early mammals competing with dinosaurs.

Animating the typically inanimate equals monsters, like tree stumps, rocks, or slime.

B. IN MEDIA

Mythic monsters come from the sea, the sky, the jungles, underground, etc.

Science spawns fearsome monsters, beginning with Dr. Frankenstein's and hitting a peak with the *Terminator*.

The atomic age ushered in a rash of 1950s movie monsters such as *Godzilla* and *Them* (giant ants). Novelist Stephen King managed to turn lots of ordinary objects into monsters, including cars and cell phones.

C. IN YOUR CREATIONS

Inner Drives Centers of Motivation – Root: death, survival.

German philosopher Friedrich Nietzsche advised, "Whoever fights monsters should see to it that in the process he does not become a monster." Show your heroine taking on some characteristic of the monster in order to defeat it. And then having trouble giving up that ability.

Update mythic monsters.

Scan science reports for new discoveries and technologies to monsterize: deep-sea creatures, deep-earth exploration, off-planet life forms, genetics, etc.

ALIENS AMONG US

I once attended a Hollywood party where the hosts had set up a black light and a recliner; you could lie down, bare your skin, and have the black light scanned over you to search for alien surgery scars, said to show up under black lights. Hey, it was Hollywood.

CHARACTERISTICS

Extraterrestrials range from human-like to the silicon-based rock monsters of *Star Trek* and *Galaxy Quest,* to the lizards of *Alien Nation* and *V,* to particular smells and shades of color.

The way we know they're alien is because their appearance, motives, or means are subtly, or wildly, different from those of humans.

A. IN ACTION

Many people claim to have encountered aliens; some claim to be aliens. Hypnotherapists claim to retrieve memories of alien abductions, including impregnations, stolen fetuses, lost time, and travel to the mother ship.

UFO conventions and websites draw huge crowds, and the U.S.

government funds the Search for Extra Terrestrial Intelligence [SETI], scanning the cosmos with telescopes and computers for signs of obviously designed signals.

Theories abound about government cover-ups of alien contact and technology. Many believe contact has been going on for eons and embrace the ancient astronauts theory of how humans and civilization came to this planet.

And yet... there's been no widely accepted, scientifically proven, repeatably testable evidence for alien contact. Again, that's good news for storytellers — imagine what you will, no one can prove you wrong.

B. IN MEDIA

Mythologies tell of visitations and genetic manipulations by extraterrestrials. Sumerian myths credit the Anunaki with creating humans as a labor force, as retold in the *Stargate* movie and series. The Bible mentions the Sons of God interbreeding with the Daughters of Men, and many interpret Ezekiel's Chariot and Jacob's Ladder as spacecraft. The ancient astronauts theories propose that the Teacher Gods of most cultures were off-planet explorers.

Scientology teaches a colonization by aliens many millions of years ago, remnants of which still attach to humans.

Invasion of the Body Snatchers embodied Cold War paranoia as humans were taken over in their sleep to become bodies for the aliens. The *Alien* movies, starring Sigourney Weaver, were exceptionally terrifying because the slathering-fanged alien looked vaguely human and used live humans as disposable nests for its vicious offspring.

The *X-Files* TV series gives exposure to all sorts of aliens and cover-up conspiracies.

Some stories reverse the trend with good aliens tut-tutting over bad humans. *The Day the Earth Stood Still* echoes the legend of teacher aliens putting a quarantine around earth after that Atlantis debacle. In the TV series *Alien Nation* conflict centers on how to integrate lizardly humanoids into regular life in LA... as if anyone would notice.

C. IN YOUR CREATIONS

Inner Drives Centers of Motivation – Variable, depending on what they are and what they want.

Let your imagination run wild!

Even if your aliens deliver your story's message, give them something to learn from humans in return.

Limit the weirdness to two to three basic concepts: faster-than-light travel, mind reading, stopping time, etc.

Go far enough back or forward in time, and human evolution looks pretty alien.

HAUNTED THINGS AND HAIR-RAISING PLACES

Things and places can be haunted. Strictly speaking, any religion's paradise and hell are haunted by no-longer-human entities. Travels to the underworld are so common in myth there's a special name for the guide – psychopomp.

Ships and buildings are ripe for haunting since humans often die in them. So are temples and tombs.

CHARACTERISTICS

Different laws of physics. Time slows or speeds up. Some hells are misty oblivion, some crowded torture. Most reflect the individual's expectations.

A. IN ACTION

Some people claim to sense former inhabitants in houses, sacred places, and battlefields — even to correctly describing them.

Legends of haunted ships have thrilled us since humans first began to float above the unknown deep. I've gone on the Halloween tour of the Queen Mary in Long Beach Harbor, featuring haunted parts of the historic ocean liner where people swear they've heard voices of long-dead crewmen.

B. IN MEDIA

Mythic heroes Ulysses, Aeneas, Hercules, Orpheus, and many others traveled to the underworld, as did Italian poet Dante in his epic, *The Divine Comedy.*

Both the Tibetan and the Egyptian *Book of the Dead* offer advice on how to navigate the afterlife, avoid demons, move to the next dimension, or get reborn. So do Mystery Schools.

The film *What Dreams May Come* showed artistically gorgeous renditions of the self-created afterlife, where some of the dead look like they did in life, while others do not.

Conan the Barbarian was always battling ghosts in haunted places. The TV series *Lost* drew watchers curious about what or who was haunting the island. The *Pirates of the Caribbean* movies feature ghostly ships and sailors.

C. IN YOUR CREATIONS

Inner Drives Centers of Motivation – Solar Plexus: the doorway to other dimensions, & Root Center: death.

Even if you're sending your character to the typical afterlife of their religion, toss in something unexpected: their cell phone works but no one can hear them, their own fears turn into monsters and turn on them, their words are taken literally, etc.

It's said that heaven is gaining your heart's desire — and so is hell. Show that reflection and polarity between the two extremes.

Exaggerate something merely annoying from real life into something fearsome in the afterlife: traffic, yappy dogs, telemarketers.

Where's the back door to Hell? What unlocks it?

The protagonist usually goes to the underworld to retrieve information, a weapon, a treasure, or a loved one. If your character does return, have them bring back something unexpected as well: a recipe, design idea, song, game, etc.

CONCLUSION

Regardless of whether you've seen ghosts, angels, or aliens... lots of people believe they have. Regardless of whether you believe in such things without seeing them... lots of people do. Humans have been filling our stories with these fascinating nonhumans since we first huddled around a campfire and turned flickering shadows into the ghosts of our ancestors.

Recall Mulder's poster in the *X-Files* TV series, "I want to believe." Most people do want to believe the weird stuff, which makes our storytelling that much easier. Just remember to hold internal logic, skew your character descriptions and actions enough to keep us off balance and uncomfortable, and maintain mystery all the way through.

∽IV∽

THE LURE OF THE DARK SIDE

So why do those people in the last section go to the

Dark Side? How do they get lured away? What are

the steps they take? These are important questions

your audience wants you to answer. It's not enough

to just give two-dimensional cut-out characters — this

guy's bad because, well, he wears the black hat; that

woman's bad because she just kidnapped the hero's

baby. Tell us why. It's scarier when you show us

how evil, darkness, and even simple dimness works

because we can then more easily imagine that there,

but for the grace of God, we might also go. Plus, it's way more entertaining to watch a temptation, decline, and fall than to just start out with a ready-made villain.

Depending on your plot structure, you may not always be showing us the full history of the villain or the situations that brought him to be that way, but by knowing this backstory well yourself, you can make potent reference to it that will enrich your portrayals. ∽

10.
THE DEVIL MADE ME DO IT

+ The ghost

+ The fatal flaw

+ I was under orders

+ Ate the Twinkies, drank the Kool-Aid

+ Gateway Dwellers

+ Guilt, grief, and shame

+ Born under a bad sign

+ Karma

+ Curses and voices

+ Aliens

Your audience wants to know *why* we do the things we do.

What turns faithful spouses into adulterers, honest people into thieves, and innocent babies into mass murderers? The Catholic Church has a catch-all answer: Original Sin. Freud identified it as inherent aggression. Superstitions blame evil curses. Reincarnationists cite karma. Whatever the cause, it's a fact that some people just simply go bad. Look what happened to that sweet little boy Anakin Skywalker.

The popularization of psychological principles moved the supernatural inside, and instead of being possessed by seven demons, a person now has Multiple Personality Disorder. Neurobiology has pinpointed regions in the brain that cause hallucinations both visual and aural, so that voice of the devil you hear may just be bad brain wiring. On the other hand, some say your brain is just the radio the devil uses to talk to you.

The first words I learned in Klingon were *Pich vighaj-BE*, "It's not my fault," a very handy phrase. Contrary to blaming everything on other people, Fate, or the gods, however, self-help systems preach a healthy responsibility for one's own actions. This can veer over into blaming others for their weaknesses, but the principle is sound.

Science may explain the mechanisms, but keep in mind the influence of archetypes and *devas*. Just as we can be swept up emotionally by love, loyalty, and joy, so too can we be swept into maelstroms of jealousy, lust, and hate. It's enough to give one pause: maybe it *is* devils, because the alternative is rather unsettling. If it's all just us humans....

This section explores some backstory and cause-and-effect reasons for why your characters go down the Left Hand Path.

THE GHOST

What is it in your character's past that haunts his present? A dead wife like in *Lethal Weapon*? A failed rescue like in *The Guardian*? A mother's tragedy over the loss of a child like in *Sophie's Choice*? The injury that scarred the *Phantom of the Opera*? Everybody has something they regret doing, or something they dearly wish had not happened. To increase suspense, reveal this motivation slowly throughout the story, and be sure it fits. Losing a kitten isn't likely to create a serial killer; losing a mother might. What will bring balance and peace for your character? Do they accept it when offered? Or are they so identified with their suffering they refuse to let it go?

THE FATAL FLAW

Every tragic character has one. Choose from your basic Seven Deadly Sins: Greed, Lust, Gluttony, Sloth, Anger, Pride, Envy. Also visit the "Dweller on the Threshold" chapter. Hubris (pride) is a typical flaw in Shakespearean drama and Greek myth. What do character flaws allow your characters to do? I heard a boisterous guy at a party say, "I was sober for three weeks. I had to start drinking again because without it, I had no excuse for my otherwise inexcusable behavior." The Fatal Flaw is usually a positive quality taken to excess; show us that process. Charlie Sheen in *Wall Street* is a good example of the progress of ambition ramping up to greed and the problems that causes. In the classic *Sunset Boulevard* it's ambition plus vanity that turn corrupt and deadly.

I WAS UNDER ORDERS

Some people excuse their actions with the Nuremberg Defense, used by Nazis in the post World War II warcrime trials: I was just following orders. Most Military Codes insist soldiers refuse to carry out illegal or inhumane orders, as do the Geneva Conventions. Wars and police actions too often provide cover and sanction for people just yearning to be bad. Show diverse approaches to these situations: refusal, reluctance, overindulgence of sadism, wavering, etc. Research the Vietnam Mai-Lai Massacre, the Zimbardo Experiment, Iraq's Abu Ghraib, and other wartime and police atrocities. Play with the concepts that "Soldiers don't make policy, politicians do," and "Guns don't kill people, people do."

ATE THE TWINKIES,™ DRANK THE KOOL-AID™

Hard to believe, but people have actually been acquitted for murder because they were under the influence of too much sugar (The Twinkie Defense). Most legal systems recognize crimes of passion and are more lenient to those possessed by the raging devil of jealousy. Mediterranean cultures typically waive crimes committed when the hot dry Sirocco winds howl in off the deserts. So far Los Angeles has not implemented a "Santa Ana wind" defense, but give us time. Until fairly recently in Texas, a man would not even be arrested for killing his wife and her lover. And there are "honor killings" in some cultures where outraged male relatives slay a girl perceived to have misbehaved.

To "drink the Kool-Aid" is to be brainwashed, as in the 1976 Jonestown Massacre where followers of cult leader Jim Jones drank poisoned Kool-Aid in a mass suicide/murder. The term is used a lot in politics and the military.

GATEWAY DWELLERS

Our Dwellers on the Threshold offer gateways to the Dark Side. Temptations, dependencies, obsessions, and addictions can get way out of hand. Some say they are gateways for the Darkness to enter a person; others that they are gateways for it to come through them and out into the world. Either way, show us how not dealing with the problem enlarges the gateway and leads to more trouble. Films such as *Barfly, Leaving Las Vegas, Postcards from the Edge, Girl Interrupted, 28 Days, Quills, In the Realm of the Senses, Last Tango in Paris*, and *Who's Afraid of Virginia Woolf* dramatize this tragic process of temporary, too often permanent, insanity.

GUILT, GRIEF, AND SHAME

These emotions are dumb, Velcro animals that rub up against you and if you're not careful, carry you along their plodding path into the Darkness. Characters need to learn that guilt, grief, and shame are signposts, not destinations. They need to get the lesson and then move on. Drama occurs when they don't. Films that show what happens when people get stuck there are *Fisher King* and *The Prince of Tides* (guilt), *Ordinary People* and *Don't Look Now* (grief), and *The Elephant Man* and Quasi Modo in *The Hunchback of Notre Dame* (shame).

BORN UNDER A BAD SIGN

Nature or nurture? Are some people just wicked from the womb? Science can almost pinpoint the places in the brain where imbalances mean a person will be a criminal of some sort. Does that take away the blame? Watch Stanley Kubrick's troubling *A Clockwork Orange* for an exploration of social engineering on born-bad boys. How will neuroscience affect our judicial system if a person can't help being who they are?

KARMA

Millions of people believe in Karma — the balancing out of actions over lifetimes. Build this into a character's belief system or your story's plot logic and you can have repercussions from the past playing out in your here-and-now. *The Fountain* does this, with Hugh Jackman in three disparate lifetimes. *Dead Again* follows a murder plot over two lifetimes. Remember there's also family Karma, cultural Karma, racial Karma, and species Karma.

CURSES AND VOICES

If your story's supernatural, then your characters can be lured or snatched into the Darkness with little regard for real-life logic. Be sure you're consistent within your own story, though. Ultra-religious people are prone to possession and can be led into Darkness by the flip side of their supposed righteousness. See more at TV Evangelists and sanctimonious politicians.

Possession is very real to many people. Research why and how it works for them; offer other explanations for the process; give us characters who buy into it and others who don't. See *The Exorcist*, *Wes Craven's New Nightmare*, *The Mummy(s)*, spooky movies, and mental patient stories for how it can work in stories. Research neuroscience for how it actually works in the brain.

ALIENS

In the Koran, the angel Gabriel removes a dark spot (the Ha'ab) from Mohammed's heart. This concept is highly effective in sci-fi stories such as the Cold War allegory *Invasion of the Body Snatchers*; *Alien*, where the demon seed grows inside your chest then violently bursts out; *The Thing*, where it commandeers your DNA; or *Babylon 5*, where the controlling aliens attach to your neck and the only way to get free is to get them dead drunk by drinking your own self silly. Show a real difference in your character before and after the takeover. Show them fighting it; or that it allows their Dark Side to finally flourish.

CONCLUSION

In many stories the antagonist is challenged to explain why she's doing all the bad things she's been doing. In *Who Killed Roger Rabbit*, slinky cartoon dame Jessica Rabbit huskily whispers that she isn't really bad, she's just drawn that way. Film noir characters offer cynical excuses. In the TV series *24*, many people doing really bad things think that's just the price they must pay to bring about good results.

In your creations, give us that moment of revelation where the character explains the whys and wherefores of her actions. The answers can be surprising, maddening, pitiful, or pathetic. Will this revelation make any difference to your protagonist? Will the antagonist change after this admission? This revelation offers an opportunity to present that bit of wisdom or wit you want us to take away from your story.

11.
DEVICES OF THE DARK SIDE

✦ Sleeping with the enemy

✦ Seemed like a good idea at the time

✦ Slippery slope

✦ Deal with the devil

✦ Power corrupts

✦ Cover your ass

✦ Violence

✦ Go along to get along

✦ Dumb and dumber

Your audience also wants to find out *how* people and things go bad.

Writers usually up the stakes by increasing the power and influence of the Villain and/or that Dangerous Situation.

This section delves into various triggers and processes that turn people bad. Sometimes it just takes a nudge; other times they must be brutalized to let go of good. For nonvillains, there are those occasions where to feed your babies or save your loved ones, an otherwise upstanding person must lie, steal, or kill; sometimes they get lured further into the Dark.

The variations are endless and the process fascinating, so show us at least some of your character's arc and reveal some of how he becomes the way he is, not to excuse his behavior, but to get us engaged in his story as well as the protagonist's. Here then are some of the ways it sometimes just all goes to heck in a handbasket.

SLEEPING WITH THE ENEMY

Since Adam took a bite from the apple Eve offered, humans have done all sorts of bad things because of love, lust, and sex. People break society's rules, leave jobs, abandon families, betray countries, lie, steal, and kill for love, or some version of it. Some relationships are so torrid and troubling, so love-hate, it can feel like the Stockholm Syndrome where hostages actually bond with their captors.

Great desire is subject to manipulation via great deception. Espionage organizations have sex schools to train agents in the arts of seduction. You'd think alpha males and femme fatales are more effective than nesting men and nice women, but that makes the latter better spies because you typically don't suspect them.

It's not unusual to hate the person you passionately desire — she makes you feel weak and addicted. Abuse and stalking can result, as well as torture and death. Crimes of passion usually get special legal treatment, akin to a plea of temporary insanity.

Love is blind, moves mountains, and can bring down kingdoms. Watch *Double Indemnity, The Night Porter, Body Heat, Dangerous Liaisons, No Way Out, In the Realm of the Senses, Monster,* and *Basic Instinct* for excellent examples of sex as the steamy road to perdition. On the lighter side, watch *Grease* where squeaky clean Olivia Newton John turns black-leather for love of bad boy John Travolta.

SEEMED LIKE A GOOD IDEA
AT THE TIME

The road to hell is paved with good intentions. It's the Law of Unintended Consequences, when one seemingly good thing causes something else to happen and that leads to another, and to another, and the eventual outcome stinks.

Military strategy sessions ideally plan for fourth- and fifth-level consequences, but are often faced with Mission Creep, when things just get bigger than you thought possible. Rabbits were introduced into Australia for sport hunting but they quickly propagated into horrific pests, destroying much of the environment. Fire-retardant asbestos is a good insulator but really bad for the lungs. The drug Thalidomide stops morning sickness but causes deformed babies. Some dams for flood control and hydroelectric power have become ecological disasters.

In *Finding Nemo* the well-meaning dentist crows that he had found Nemo struggling for life and saved him, but the little fish was effectively kidnapped, and both he and his dad had to brave many dangers to get him back home. In the film *Under Fire* photojournalist Nick Nolte fakes live pictures of a dead leader to shore up the Nicaraguan rebels and keep American support, but his actions lead to the death of many others, including his good friend Gene Hackman.

Have your characters either not see or willfully ignore the unintended consequences of their seemingly good ideas, and remember the old saying, "No good deed goes unpunished."

THE SLIPPERY SLOPE

From the little white lie to Hitler, from the Prince of Dimness to Darth Vader, once you set foot on the Left Hand Path it's a slippery slope with little hope of return. Most cautionary tales begin with the single misstep; usually the audience knows it's a bad idea but the protagonist either doesn't know, thinks it's inconsequential, or is in a state of denial.

Sitcoms are mostly about someone telling a fib and then getting deeper and deeper entangled in the repercussions. Geoffrey Rush in *The Tailor of Panama* fabricates the truth about local intrigue in ways that quickly get out of hand, bringing in the British Secret Service and ultimately a U.S. military invasion. In the Wachowski brothers' *Bound*, lesbian sexual straying leads to larceny and mob murders. Other films using this device are *Wall Street* about ambition and greed, *The Hunger* about a reporter's curiosity about vampirism, *Badlands* about a young girl's fascination with a bad boy, *Heart of Darkness* about European colonial rule in the Congo, and *Apocalypse Now* about a military commander in Viet Nam taking on god-like powers.

Marijuana is called a gateway drug to the hard stuff, though the evidence is sketchy and many recreational users never go beyond pot. Likewise, people who experiment with a bit of bondage may never get into hardcore S&M, and taking a drink needn't lead to alcoholism. But stories are ever so much more interesting when they do.

This downhill ride can be quite hypnotic. It begins with the initial bite, then the denial, the larger crime, the cover-up, the grip of guilt, giving up any remaining inclination to do good, hardening the heart, and embracing evil. Create effective drama by focusing on three or more of these steps. How is someone lured into the first step? In most of the mentioned films, there's someone already there who guides or lures the protagonist in via charisma. What's the "gateway drug" of the setup: sex, money, position, knowledge? What's at stake: reputation, marriage, career, life? Why is the cover-up worse than the crime? Show how the thing snowballs and is soon unmanageable.

A DEAL WITH THE DEVIL

Sometimes people just decide to make a deal with the devil and sell their souls for some great desire. They know it's wrong, they know it's risky, but they do it anyway.

Ordinary people's jealousy often attributes this device to people with extraordinary accomplishments: Simon Magus from the New Testament, 13th-century alchemist Roger Bacon, 19th-century composer and violin virtuoso Nicolo Paganini. Legend has it guitarist Robert Johnson met the devil at the crossroads and sold his soul to become the greatest blues musician ever.

Dr. Faustus sells his soul to Mephistopheles. In some versions it's for sex and power, in others for knowledge. At the end of the former he's whisked down to hell, but in the latter he's redeemed for having had the courage to search for deep answers.

Though the Dark Brotherhood can supposedly defer their personal Karma from lifetime to lifetime, for a regular human who makes a deal with the devil, it may be "No money down and no interest," but there's always a huge and horrid balloon payment at the end. Show us that, as in Mozart's opera "Don Giovanni," where the villainous seducer sinks through the dining room floor directly into hell, and in Oscar Wilde's *A Portrait of Dorian Gray*, where the portrait had been aging instead of the man.

POWER CORRUPTS

Julius Caesar, today's news, your big brother, your bitchy boss — we've all seen lots of examples of power getting out of hand when in the wrong hands. Sometimes the corruption is petty, like security guards with badges and guns. Sometimes it's deadly, like Hitler, Pol Pot, and tribal warlords.

There's a little something in all of us that wants to be right, to be in charge, to be in the spotlight. The more we feel wronged or ignored, the more desirous we are of power to balance that out, and the more dangerous we are if we actually get that power and there's no one around who can or will stop us.

The movie *Viva Zapata* opens with barefoot hat-in-hand peasant Marlon Brando being rejected by a corrupt official behind a big desk. After leading a successful revolution and falling prey to the lure of power, the movie ends with now corrupted Brando behind the same big desk, rejecting the pleas of a barefoot hat-in-hand peasant. Political reformers often fall prey to the same process.

In *Jesus Christ Superstar,* Judas complains that Jesus is a glory hog, inflated by the power of his celebrity. The Masterpiece Theatre series *I, Claudius* is an excellent study in the abuse of power among Roman Emperors, even to apotheosis – declaring themselves gods. Throughout history, king-as-god has corrupted many a throne.

As an artist you're probably not primarily driven by power, so you might well wonder, "Is power enough of a motivator?" The mystic explanation is that when *prana* (life force) is flowing through the Lower Solar Plexus, the Center of personal power, it feeds the energy needs of the entire body and is very, very invigorating. The sense of being super-alive is exhilarating, particularly for someone who hasn't felt it before. This dynamic has been the downfall of many an artist through self-importance and greed.

Your character arc could begin with any of these: powerlessness, feeling dead inside, being used by others, lacking or being denied something greatly desired.

Show a character flaw that isn't so awful, mostly because there is no opportunity to pursue it, e.g. fine food, kinky sex, fast cars. Once she gains power, the character swells with explosive self-importance and the flaw goes wild; like plugging a toaster directly into a power pole, the overload bursts through those weak spots and wreaks havoc.

Redemption for the power-corrupted could be an expansion of your character's concern and care for others, even at some cost to himself. Or, just have someone or some thing finally stop him, legally or illegally, verbally or violently.

COVER YOUR ASS

It's not the crime, it's the cover-up. Lots of people get snared deeper in the Dark Side while trying to escape blame or punishment. People turn stool pigeon and rat out their buddies to save their own skin, hence the Witness Protection Program.

Texans joke there are only two rules for politics: 1) Don't get caught, and 2) If you do get caught, turn State's Evidence.

Cover-ups compound the crime and escalate the consequences: President Nixon and the Watergate burglary, President Reagan and Iran-Contra, AIDS in many countries, bird flu in China, the Bush Administration's outing of CIA agent Valerie Plame, and many more.

VIOLENCE

Abuse breaks something in the human soul which once broken, can seldom be repaired. The Dark Side uses those sharp fragments to create more pain by harming others, passing on the pattern to one's children, or turning on one's self with disgust, shame, or the desire to escape at any cost.

Sometimes people are literally forced to be bad. Children kidnapped and turned into soldiers is a horrid but real example. Books by and about African child soldiers recount being "turned" by being forced to kill family members and other children, being made sex slaves to adult soldiers, and being thrust into battle.

Though there is an instinctual cruelty in children, it's usually socialized out by positive upbringing and the wiring for empathy that occurs around ages three to five. However, those who gleefully inflict pain and torture at an early age seldom give it up. Whether it's bad brain wiring or any of the other possible causes, children who torture animals or other people — physically, emotionally, or mentally — usually grow up to perfect those Dark skills.

As psychological experiments have shown, we all have a sadistic streak and when given free rein, many of us indulge it. Look into Dr. Zimbardo's famous Stanford Prison Experiment and its relevance to the Abu Ghraib prison scandals for insights into situational evil, where it's probably the bad barrel rather than the bad apples causing the problem.

Sometimes instinctual blood lust kicks in as in *Bloodsport* or *Fight Club* (or self-defense as in *Carrie*), but often it's a cold-blooded fixation. Different from the Slippery Slope paradigm, this is more a hunger-for-more. Talk to anyone who'll admit having done something bad while knowing it was bad but kept on with it, and you'll pick up a fascination for the lure of power and pain. Investigate China's Cultural Revolution, *The Killing Fields*, *Kiss of the Spider Woman*, and the TV series *24* for more details.

GO ALONG TO GET ALONG

Allowing evil to occur makes you partly to blame for whatever happens. In a landmark case from the 1970s, New Yorker Kitty Genovese repeatedly screamed for help, but 18 people in the middle-class neighborhood didn't want to get involved, and the young woman was knifed to death.

Many schools and military academies hold responsible anyone who knows about cheating and doesn't report it.

Most of the world ignored the Rwanda genocide and were slow to move into Darfur, some say because the people are black and there are no valuable resources in the area. Many Turks still deny the Armenian Genocide of the early 1900s, and some people deny the deadliest example, the Nazi Holocaust, wherein millions were exterminated.

Excuses are, "It's always been that way," "You can't fight City Hall," "I'm just one person," "It's none of my business," and

"Forget it, Jake, it's Chinatown," from the Robert Towne film starring Jack Nicholson as a detective uncovering corruption about LA's water supply.

Whistle-blowers are the heroes of this category. The U.S. has laws to protect them, and *Time* magazine once made three whistle-blowers Persons of the Year. Movies about this device of the Dark Side include *The Insider, Silkwood, The Constant Gardener, Road to Perdition, Prince of the City, LA Confidential,* and *Chinatown.*

DUMB AND DUMBER

Remember those Bumblers from "Bad Boys and Girls"? Sometimes people are simply too stupid to realize what's going on, like teenagers who have sex in the spooky woods where six of their friends just got massacred by a slasher who's still on the loose. People who take ridiculous chances in sports or homemade stunts and people who're careless with fire and sharp edges are open to Dark Side dangers. Blithely ignoring the warning signs from bad people or dangerous situations, as well as ignoring actual signs, gets people into lots of trouble. And for those nude photos that turn up once someone's a celebrity? "I was young and I needed the money." The Dumb(er) device is mostly used in comedies and the horror genre.

CONCLUSION

The Dark Side has many devices to lure people onto the Left Hand Path. Use these processes to add depth to your villains, pathos to your heroes, and danger to your story situations.

V

CONFRONTING THE DARK SIDE

If we were at Harry Potter's Hogwarts School we'd float off to a class on Defenses Against the Dark Arts. But your heroes need to battle more than just wicked wizards, they need to go up against everything life and beyond can throw at them. No matter the genre or style, once the conflict has been engaged, once the heroine is on the journey, the rest of your story is all about confronting the Dark: her own Dwellers on the Threshold; the Dark Forces of inertia, time, etc.; or the really big bad guys. No matter what form any of that takes — a seduction, an abduction, a deluge, a demon, or a diabolical corporation — we relish watching our heroine go up against the forces of evil.

12.
DEFENSE AGAINST THE DARK SIDE

+ Charms and chants

+ Therapy, drugs, self-help

+ Ignore it

+ Laughter

+ Education

+ Deception and diplomacy

+ Exposure

+ Nonviolence

+ Civil disobedience

+ Fight fire with fire

+ You say you want a revolution?

+ Cut to the chase

+ Seek sanctuary

+ Trials, truths, and reconciliations

+ The Primrose Path

+ The Road to Damascus

+ Get a sense of perspective

There are as many philosophies about how to combat the Dark Side as there are explanations for how it came about. That's good news because you've then got worlds and times enough from which to draw your inspiration and examples.

In this section we'll explore diverse ways people have fought the Darkness within and without. Winning is great, but sometimes losing is more effective dramatically. Ancient Greeks used this approach with *Oedipus Rex*, a man who mistakenly kills his father and marries his mother, and with the cursed Atriedes family who indulge in vengeful cannibalism. Then there's Shakespeare's *Hamlet, Othello, MacBeth,* and more. Though with a note of hope, *Gone With the Wind* ends sadly with carpetbaggers invading the South and Scarlett separated from Rhett.

Whether your story ends happily, tragically, or leaves us wondering, we demand an exciting struggle up to that point. So check out this list, choose your weapons, and let the battles begin.

CHARMS AND CHANTS

In our search for order and meaning, and realizing our own frailty against time and nature, humans often call for outside assistance. The ancients read goat guts before setting out to battle. Tombs in Egypt contain scores of blue glass figurines, thought to be protective talismans; however, some think they're batteries: Imagine if modern batteries were shaped like pink bunnies. A common figure across the Middle East and North Africa is the open hand with an eye in the palm to guard against the Evil Eye.

Magic of the Caribbean involves icons made more powerful if they contain bits of the person to be spelled or cursed, such as hair, nail clippings, or clothes. Some Buddhist shrines have digits or hair from Buddha, just as some Catholic Churches have reliquaries (special containers) containing body parts (relics) of their saints.

Esoteric science explains that the vibration of something is carried in all its parts, so like a remote-activated chip, or a baby-minder walkie-talkie in the nursery, you can take the connection with you, or transmit power from afar. Whatever the mechanics or effectiveness, we love our charms and chants and continue to use them for protection.

A. IN ACTION

In post-WWII Philippines, American Colonel Lansdale used their own superstitions against the Huk rebels. Playing on local lore, rumors were spread that a soothsayer was predicting "men with evil in their hearts" would fall prey to the *asuang* (vampire). American troops then lay in wait for a passing Huk patrol and snatched away the last fellow in line. His neck received two puncture wounds and he was bled to death. The blood-drained corpse was placed back on the trail for the returning Huk patrol to find. News of vampire attacks spread, and support for the rebels fell off dramatically in that area.

In many cultures, a typical protective charm is to symbolically cut you up, toss you in a bubbling cauldron of magic brew, and when you come out all in one piece again, you are invincible. (Some people try to reenact this with tequila, but the results are dubious.) This is similar to Achilles' mom dipping him in the river Styx, all except for his heel. The Catholic Church uses Holy Water for regular blessings as well as for exorcisms.

Today in Africa, some soldiers get rubbed with magic oil or have their bullets blessed so they'll be invincible — despite all evidence to the contrary.

B. IN MEDIA

Talismans and magic weapons feature in the earliest myths, be it Thor's hammer or Athena's invisible helmet. Zombie, werewolf, and vampire movies use charms and crosses, silver bullets, and wooden stakes. Charmed swords such as King Arthur's Excalibur show up in fantasy and action-adventure stories.

The Mummy and *Scorpion King* movies use ancient Egyptian curses and talismans. A St. Christopher medal was significant in the 2006 Oscar-winning movie *Crash*.

In the TV series *Charmed* and *Buffy the Vampire Slayer*, characters use charms, spells, and concoctions to counter the Dark Side, though sometimes they themselves misuse them and go bad.

Sword-and-sorcery games, movies, and books run on spells and magic. In the *Age of Mythology* game you can send villagers to worship and receive god-points. See the "Witches, Warlocks and Wizards" chapter for more details.

C. IN YOUR CREATIONS

Inner Drives Center of Motivation - Solar Plexus: connection to the astral/emotional planes.

Unless you're using a very familiar talisman such as a cross, you'll need to show us its connection to the power source. In the book and movie *Nightwatch,* the spiked dog collar that protected Anton from the Dark Side came straight off the neck of the Dark Side Biggie.

Have your heroine follow Colonel Lansdale's lead and use the enemy's beliefs as weapons against them; it's cheaper and easier.

Put a time limit on the effectiveness of your chant/charm, or maybe it only works when a child holds it, when the moon is full, or only with the right magic words. These items are like software programs: they must be used absolutely correctly or they simply won't work at all.

Make sure the talisman remains a tool the heroine uses and not a *deus ex machina*, as that would drain power from your heroine.

If your story is really scary or tragic or follows the Pygmalion-Frankenstein theme, having the stuff go wild and take over is quite appropriate.

Throw out the laws of physics and have fun — or scare us silly.

THERAPY, DRUGS, SELF-HELP

Given that your characters aren't actually possessed by demons (though they may claim to be), these treatments can be effective on Dwellers on the Threshold such as getting caught up in a cult, suffering from Post Traumatic Stress Disorder (PTSD), depression, multiple personalities, etc.

Ancient disciplines used meditation and mantras, confessions and penance, special exercises and diets — all intended to change body chemistry and, hence, the mind, emotions, and actions. Modern science offers quicker tools via chemistry. But the change has got to occur in consciousness before it'll stick; "acting as if" only goes so far.

There's a concept that all illness is psychological and one's physical condition just reflects one's consciousness. The good news here is we have free choice to select perfect health, abundance, joyous relationships, etc. The bad news is that if we are not manifesting those, it's our own fault. This viewpoint fails to take into account simple physics and inertia of the stuff of the world. For most of us, changing our attitude about a disease or situation will not necessarily bring overnight changes: there is a lot of heavy resistance out there.

A. IN ACTION

Exorcisms can fall in this category or the previous one about charms, depending on the belief system. The Catholic Church still trains Exorcists, Western-based Scientology and Eastern-based

DEFENSE AGAINST THE DARK SIDE

Okyomi both claim to remove "attaching spirits," called *dybbuks* by Jewish Rabbis also trained in removing them.

Bio-feedback, talk therapy, and support teams produce good results in helping people deal with their Dwellers. Antidepressants have a dicey record of helping many but addicting others. Some claim they've caused suicides.

Confessional radio and TV shows offer public forums to release one's inner demons, but ewwwwwww.

Combat veterans, survivors of natural disasters, and people involved in violent situations are vulnerable to PTSD. Esoterically it's said these people's *etheric* bodies have been shattered and must be repaired. Eastern medicine addresses this with acupuncture and other energy-balancing techniques.

B. IN MEDIA

Girl Interrupted, 21 Days, Sybil, The Three Faces of Eve, and *The Sopranos* all feature therapy. The TV series *House* centers on a misanthropic doctor addicted to pain pills.

On the funny side are the movies *Postcards from the Edge, High Anxiety, Analyze This/That,* and TV's *Monk,* an obsessive-compulsive who solves mysteries.

Long-running TV series *Frasier* featured a talk-show shrink, TV psych Dr. Phil offers tough-love advice, and real-life trash-TV confessor Jerry Springer even inspired an opera(?!). Then again, the best opera poster I ever saw read: Men cheat, women cry, people die — that's opera.

C. IN YOUR CREATIONS

Inner Drives Center of Motivation – Lower Solar Plexus: issues of identity, individuation, and psychic phenomenon.

Therapy is usually like peeling an onion: Each layer reveals a new wound or misconception. Chart revelations about your character's problem with increasingly disturbing aspects, leading to a painful core wound. *Ordinary People* and *Equus* both investigate a troubled teenage boy with serious mother issues.

The complex relationship between therapist and patient is dramatic by its very nature; plus, it offers opportunity for conflicting perspectives on the same events. Recall the famous scene in *Annie Hall* when Diane Keaton tells her shrink they have sex constantly — at least three times a week – and Woody Allen tells his they hardly ever have sex — only three times a week.

Show the effects of a character's treatment on people around him as he changes and confronts his inner demons, his persecutors, and the status quo.

In a supernatural story, reveal how identity issues and letting down one's barriers via alcohol or drugs can open the doors to possession.

IGNORE IT

Recognition creates relationship, so sometimes ignoring something can actually be effective. This tactic usually works best with merely annoying but not dangerous people. It doesn't work at all with the Dark Forces: ignoring gravity, fire, or time can hurt.

Detachment and harmlessness ("Be in the world but not of it") are central tenets in Buddhism, Christianity, Wicca, and many other spiritual systems. Self-improvement gurus advise us to turn our attentions away from what we do not want to continue experiencing.

Ignoring things can sometimes work, but too often this tactic is simply naïve and ineffective, like the child covering her eyes and saying, "You know I can't see you, so don't pretend you're there."

A. IN ACTION

"Whatever..." is the quintessential, maddening word of dismissal.

The challenge of many unions and social change movements is simply to get recognized by the rulers, since public policies often ignore the unaccepted and disadvantaged, hoping they'll disappear.

Common wisdom is not to negotiate with terrorists lest you validate their existence or their cause.

New states strive to be officially "recognized" so they can do business in the broader world. Likewise, withholding validation via licensing can doom an out-of-the-mainstream movement, such as healing practices.

The U.S. military developed invisibility cloaks that take images of what's in front of you, then project that on onto your back, so it looks like you're not there at all.

B. IN MEDIA

Greek hero Perseus used a magical helmet of invisibility to sneak up on the gorgon Medusa and slay her.

The Romulan cloaking device was a favorite *Star Trek* counter-weapon, and the *Star Wars* Jedi Knights are trained in illusion — those are not the droids you're looking for.

A charming ignore-reality character is Jimmy Stewart with his giant white rabbit in *Harvey*. In *The Mists of Avalon* the ancient fairy world fades as people's attentions turn towards Christianity.

Dr. Pangloss in Voltaire's satire *Candide* believes "All is for the best in this best of all possible worlds." Similar airhead characters include *Pollyanna*, Edith Bunker from *All in the Family* '70s TV series, Karen in *Will & Grace*, and Joey in *Friends*. Cynics note this may indeed be the best possible world.

C. IN YOUR CREATIONS

Inner Drives Center of Motivation - Aspirational Solar Plexus: "It's all good."

Since individuals do create their own reality by interpreting actual reality, show different characters interpreting the same events in very different ways.

Give us three to five steps in the progression as a character greatly troubled by a problem or a person first disengages and becomes more detached, until they are finally free of the old habit or old boyfriend — or not. If not, show them trying and why it does not work.

Show how sometimes a positive attitude really can change reality by altering other people's attitudes and actions.

Illustrate the downside of not facing reality.

Demonstrate that the first "No" is the best "No" by showing what happens when you do engage with something rather than ignoring it. Then have your character face a similar situation and with what she's learned, do better.

Define the boundary of effectiveness for your character's attitude: works on fellow students, not on teachers; works on people, not on thunderstorms; works for a short while, then consensus reality prevails.

LAUGHTER

Activist Saul Alinski advised that ridicule is man's most potent weapon. It infuriates bullies to be laughed at because it trivializes them. If driven by low self esteem in the first place, to plug right into that weakness may eventually deflate them to impotence.

Tyrants use fear to manipulate others. If you remove their fear tools, they become ineffective. Of course, it's hard to laugh at a foolish dictator who still has the power to kill you.

Humor saves our sanity in times of Darkness. It's a measure of our humanity that very quickly after a disaster, the jokes begin. The 1986 space shuttle Challenger disaster spawned morbid jokes just a few days after it exploded and plunged into the sea. 9/11 took a bit longer because of the impending shadow of more hits and rabidly serious patriotism, but it was perhaps five weeks after irony was declared "dead forever" that jokes started reappearing.

A. IN ACTION

Zen *koans* use absurdities to break through analysis-paralysis: What is the sound of one hand clapping?

Court jesters, always poking fun at the pretensions of power, were a clever immunization device against royal hubris, presuming the royals listened and learned.

In Robert Graves' *I, Claudius* novels, many autocratic Roman emperors were pathetic jokes to the people, yet because of their extreme power, fear ruled. Some assassinations seemed fueled by palace guards fed up with being laughed at by the people, particularly around Caligula and Nero.

Speakers often begin with a joke to open the audience's minds and hearts. Medical science has shown us that the physical act of laughing releases feel-good endorphins.

The theater of the absurd, satire, and irony have always been used to bring down the self-important or oblivious. Editorial cartoons lance hot-air politicians and pretentious *artistes* are flummoxed by audience laughter at their "serious" art.

B. IN MEDIA

The Producers and that quirky tune "Springtime for Hitler," the TV series *Hogan's Heroes, Young Frankenstein,* the *Scary Movie* series, *Dogma,* and *Patch Adams* apply humor to traditionally humorless situations. In the old Saturday morning cartoons the good cat/mouse/roadrunner used slap-stick humor to defeat the bad dog/cat/coyote.

The Daily Show, Saturday Night Live's newscasts, and media pundits all wield humor as socio-political weapons.

Stand-up comics and some sitcoms poke fun at societal conventions. And then there's *The Simpsons* and *South Park,* which absolutely skewer them.

The Hitchhiker's Guide to the Galaxy, Terry Pratchet's *Disk World,* and *Borat* all satirize social systems.

C. IN YOUR CREATIONS

Inner Drives Center of Motivation – Throat: cleverness.

Humor is about exaggeration, so select some trait of the baddie to mock and caricature. Laughter is contagious; once fearsome is turned into funny, the baddie's power will soon erode.

Laughter seldom converts a bully, but it can convert their followers. Once they're an object of ridicule, it's hard for a baddie to make a comeback.

On the flip side, laughter can seriously backfire, as evidenced by bullied teens who eventually fight back with weapons, to the death.

As an antidote for down-in-the-dumps characters or those paralyzed by doubt or fear, use laughter to bring them back to action. Optimism might be a reach, but you can at least get them moving again.

EDUCATION

Teaching people how to learn, to have critical thinking skills, to understand logic and cause and effect are not guarantees against falling to the Dark Side, but it is hard to manipulate people who think rather than just feel.

At least learn to recognize when you're being manipulated, seduced, or scammed, and then if you want to go along, fine. But let the manipulator know you know what they're doing, so even though they make the sale or get the kiss, you've defused their sense of power and taken away the thrill of conquest. Will they totally reform? Probably not. Have you caused a crack in their system? Maybe.

A. IN ACTION

Many cultures have myths about Teacher Gods who brought knowledge and skills, helping people move up the path of civilization. Greek centaur Chiron taught heroes Jason, Perseus, Hercules, and others the ways of war and wisdom.

Education level is a major factor in financial success and quality of life. Aid policies are moving from just giving hungry people fish to teaching them to fish and providing the opportunity to earn a fishing pole. Small business loans and mentoring help raise people from poverty to compete in markets; an originator of micro-loans won the 2006 Nobel Peace Prize.

Oppressors hit intellectuals first, burn books, and close schools — for good reason. On the seal of the University of Texas at Austin is *Disciplina Praesidium Civitatis*: education is the safeguard of democracy.

In classical Greece a well-rounded education included Grammar, Rhetoric (public speaking), Logic, Arithmetic, Geometry, Astronomy, and Music. The Renaissance Man was expected to know all these plus a number of languages, be athletic, a great dancer, and a capable warrior. The ideal modern liberal education would include all these, but seldom does.

B. IN MEDIA

The Ageless Wisdom predicts the next battle for the soul of humanity will be on the mental planes, with those who can really think manipulating those who only feel. Some say it's already happening.

Often the problem isn't Evil, it's Idiocy. In *Sleeping Beauty* the King and Queen breech court protocol by not inviting the wicked fairy. The expected revenge occurs. Years later the three airhead good fairies are stupid enough to leave Briar Rose alone just minutes before it was prophesied she'd fall under the spell. Hadn't they been paying attention the last sixteen years? A little common sense would have gone a long way here.

My Fair Lady, Educating Rita, Stand and Deliver, and *Freedom Writers* all show how learning improves dignity and quality of life.

Erin Brockovich shows a young woman educating herself to bring and win a legal challenge against a huge business. Jeff Goldblum in *Independence Day* uses his techno-smarts to give the aliens a computer virus and save the world.

Though they used plenty of firepower too, the main tactic in *The Matrix* was using the system against itself with smart cyber-sabotage. The TV series *MacGyver* focused on wit as the hero saved the day with simple tools.

The Sims games teach players to create balanced lives and societies, and *Spore* teaches how to guide evolution and create civilizations. Serious games are a huge industry, instructing people on topics from war to medicine.

C. IN YOUR CREATIONS

Inner Drives Center of Motivation – Throat: developing the intellect.

Whether your protagonist is battling an inner Dweller, a Dark Force, or some super-powerful antagonist, show how his ignorance is a drawback.

Critical thinking skills include recognizing the framing of an issue. If you start with "homeland security," a good thing to have, then whatever you put inside that is more acceptable to most people. Take away that frame, and it's a different story. Show the protagonist reframing the antagonist's stance and showing others how to resee things.

Show the sacrifice a person must make to get knowledge and acquire skills: time, friends, money, approval of peers, etc.

Most people get cocky when they're learning new things. Put your hero through that annoying know-it-all stage.

Illustrate the joy of learning, the thrill when the lights go on in the mind.

Also show how education won't always save the day and sometimes gets you killed, like in Nazi Germany, Communist China, and Pol Pot's Cambodia.

DECEPTION AND DIPLOMACY

Einstein observed that you must rise above a conflict and get some insight into the larger situation in order to solve it. This scientific principle is at work in diplomacy, arbitration, counseling, and many mediation techniques.

Animals in the wild use distraction to lead predators away from their babies. Decoys are a typical combat tactic, particularly in guerilla war. Camouflage is natural deception: leopard spots, zebra stripes, faking an accent, or wearing local clothes. But it can back-fire. Know how to kill a chameleon? Toss it in a box of crayons.

Propaganda and advertising use distraction and deception to alter perception and action. Making your enemy think you're more dangerous than you really are can be effective. A military friend tells the story of a buddy of his who woke up to a knife at her throat; she deflected the rape by telling the attacker she had all sorts of STDs. It probably helped that she was wearing Army issue boxer shorts at the time.

A. IN ACTION

In Greek myth, Jason was supposed to fight a whole crowd of war-riors alone. He tossed a stone in their midst, and when they turned against each other, Jason slew them all.

In WWII the Allies had an entire tank battalion made of cardboard and camo paint which they moved around by hand; it kept Nazi resources tied up in that part of France.

Former U.S. President Jimmy Carter uses diplomatic skills to broker peace. The United Nations, European Union, Association of Southeast Asian Nations (ASEAN), African Union (AU), and other groups apply diplomacy and public policy towards development and protection of their regions.

Sanctions are often imposed to promote acceptable behavior. This carrot-and-stick diplomatic approach worked to help end apartheid in South Africa, but it seems ineffective in Burma, Iran, Korea, and Saddam's Iraq.

B. IN MEDIA

Scheherazade deceived the wife-killing king of Persia into keep-ing her alive for yet another story. Legend says they lived happily ever after, and we got the fabulous tales in her *One Thousand and One Nights.*

Most mythologies have a Trickster who outwits stronger, more powerful enemies. Deceptively disheveled TV detective *Columbo* is a perfect trickster, using his shambling ways to get the guilty to drop their guard.

Laurence Durrell's *Alexandria Quartet,* along with Graham Greene's and Somerset Maugham's stories (many made into films), revolve on deception and back-channel diplomacy. Duplicitous love, lust, and power are usually involved.

Most spy stories, but not James Bond - that's pure action. *The Year of Living Dangerously, The Tailor of Panama, The Last Emperor, Mission Impossible,* and much of the *Dune* novels.

C. IN YOUR CREATIONS

Inner Drives Center of Motivation – Throat: mental manipulation, clever speech.

Show how the clever one came by their talent: making peace on the playground, deceiving parents, appreciating stories, etc.

Establish that the clever one often gets in trouble for speaking out or for being devious. Make it a detriment in the beginning, but it pays off at the end.

Why is secrecy essential? Show bad things happening to someone who reveals too much.

Blackmail is a battle tactic. Though they were both in the wrong, Judi Dench's character in *Notes on a Scandal* used it to get Cate Blanchett to stop her illegal affair with a minor, or so she thought.

Most people see what they want to see or expect to see. Manipulate their perceptions and you alter their reality, as was so successfully done in *The Sixth Sense.*

If you can't beat 'em, join 'em. Not really, but make them think you have. Your character then becomes a rat in the pipes and can effect lots of damage, like a counter-espionage mole.

Use the "Chomsky answer" (after linguist Noam Chomsky). Q: "Who gave you those flowers?" A: "Aren't they gorgeous? I just love yellow. What's your favorite color?" Most people don't notice they didn't get a real answer; clever people catch the deflection and keep questioning.

EXPOSURE TO LIGHT

Sunlight disinfects. Exposing dark doings often ends them, sometimes via shame, sometimes via public outrage.

Certain activities are more properly and politely done in private (personal hygiene, sex, and developing light-sensitive film), but when people meet in secret to decide or do things that affect others, they've usually got something to hide.

The press is supposed to be the instrument of investigation to bring transparency to public activities. Governments and special interest groups often try to control the media; when they succeed, people usually suffer. The Internet provides such universal access and transparency that it's difficult to keep anything private anymore (more's the pity sometimes).

Sometimes therapy helps people shine light on their own Dwellers, revealing formerly unconscious actions. Hypnotherapy can also be effective but is not totally reliable because of suggestibility.

A. IN ACTION

The Watergate political scandal and trials of the early 1970s brought down American President Richard Nixon (*All the President's Men*), and most major players served prison time. The

Iran-Contra hearings of the 1980s exposed the U.S. government's illegal involvement in selling arms to Iran and sending the money to Contras in Nicaragua. Major players went unpunished, including President Ronald Regan and V.P. George H.W. Bush.

After the Berlin Wall and the Iron Curtain went down, "transparency" was all the rage in early 1990s international politics. Storytellers feared the end of the Cold War meant we'd have no major conflicts to write about anymore... what were we thinking?!

When gigantic energy company Enron's duplicitous illegal dealings were revealed, the entire house of cards crashed, taking with it one of the (formerly) most prestigious accounting and consulting firms in the world, Arthur Andersen.

Pedophile scandals have rocked but not ruined the Catholic Church.

B. IN MEDIA

Some sex offenders, prostitute's johns, and other criminals get unwanted exposure on billboards, the Internet, and TV shows such as *America's Most Wanted*.

Exposure didn't end wrongdoing, but Jack Nicholson's detective work in *Chinatown* revealed water theft on a major scale and incest on a tragic personal scale. *LA Confidential* exposed police corruption, *The Insider* exposed tobacco company corruption, *Prince of the City* exposed justice system corruption, and *Silkwood* exposed industrial corruption. *Beyond Honor* exposes female genital mutilation in America.

Documentaries are effective light sources to shine in dark corners. *The Smartest Guys in the Room* explores the Enron energy scandal, *Who Killed the Electric Car?* questions the anti-green manipulations of big oil and big auto, and Michael Moore's films *Columbine* and *Fahrenheit 911* pose questions about America's gun culture and administration complicity and incompetence in the 9/11 events. Al Gore's *An Inconvenient Truth* raises awareness about climate change as well as business and government's resistance to dealing with it.

C. IN YOUR STORIES

Inner Drives Centers of Motivation – Sacral and Lower Solar Plexus: corruption over money, sex, and power. Throat: intellectual detective work is required to expose it.

Give your protagonist early suspicions, but then have them release the doubts as an antagonist makes reasonable explanations. Then have a slip-up that piques the protagonist back into action.

A turncoat from the Dark Side can provide the crowbar to pry up the lid on wrongdoings. Reveal why they're defecting: revenge, money, cutting a deal with the D.A., or an attack of conscience.

Like lifting a rock and watching the creepy-crawlies scramble, lifting the lid on dark doings provides action and heated dialogue with denials, finger-pointing, squealing on comrades, turning state's evidence, payoffs, and deaths.

Show a seemingly innocent bystander who knew about the dark deeds but kept quiet; how do they justify their non-actions? Did they actually condone it? Were they afraid of whistle-blowing?

Whistle-blowers and investigative reporters are heroes of exposes, and *Time* magazine's 2002 People of the Year. But show how some people do public good for private gain.

Remember, anyone attempting to hide their activities will use decoys and have plausible deniability (a good alibi).

Show the difference between "doing good" versus "being seen to be doing good." Governments often publicly pledge millions for aid and assistance, then never actually release the funds.

NONVIOLENCE

A folktale warns not to wrestle with the tar baby because you'll just get caught up in the mess. Given the typically violent aspects of human nature, nonviolence stands out as a unique defense against the Dark Side, sometimes against bullies, usually against war or oppression. Aggression often depends on resistance for excitement and fulfillment; refusal to engage can sometimes defuses that aggression.

It takes moral courage to stay nonviolent in a conflict situation and that offers a rich opportunity to explore your characters' philosophies, hopes, and weaknesses.

A. IN ACTION

Some Buddhists and all Jains refuse to harm any living thing. Quakers, Amish, and Jehovah's Witnesses philosophically resist violence. In many countries Conscientious Objectors can get non-combat assignments, and some are totally excused from military service.

Mahatma Gandhi transformed a Hindu philosophy of peace into a sweeping political movement that helped free India from British rule in the late 1940s.

Early Vietnam antiwar protests were characterized by sit-ins, love-ins, and blossoms-into-gun barrels as Flower Power helped bring American war power to a halt.

Dr. Martin Luther King Jr. urged nonviolent means for the American Civil Rights Movement, though followers didn't always hold that line. South Africa's Nelson Mandela lived nonviolent resistance at great personal cost, and Burma's Aung San Suu Kyi still does. Many former Israeli soldiers are turning officially nonviolent and leading a growing peace movement for the Israeli-Palestinian conflict.

Conflict Resolution is a real profession, using nonviolent techniques.

B. IN MEDIA

Pat Barker's award-winning *Regeneration* novels about shell-shocked (now called PTSD) World War I soldiers under psychiatric care delves into the complexities of nonviolence, honor, and the horrors of war.

Friendly Persuasion is about a Quaker family affected by the American Civil War. The biopic *Gandhi* documents the inner and outer workings of India's great national hero. *Cry Freedom* is about black antiapartheid, nonviolent leader Steve Biko.

Some come to nonviolence because they're sick and tired of being mired in violence. In the BBC series *Cadfael* an English Crusader becomes a peaceful, mystery-solving monk. Tom Cruise plays a real-life wounded Viet vet turned war protestor in *Born on the Fourth of July*. In *The Mission* Spanish knight and slaver Robert De Niro tries to become a nonviolent monk in penance for killing his own brother, but when the pressure is on, takes up the sword, this time to defend the innocent. At the core of the exceptionally violent *Passion of the Christ* is Jesus' nonviolence.

C. IN YOUR CREATIONS

Inner Drives Center of Motivation – Aspirational Solar Plexus: concern for the greater good, & Heart: self-sacrifice.

Developmental psychology notes the stages we grow through, some of which include verbal or physical violence necessary to break into our next phase, like chicks pecking through a shell or butterflies struggling out of the cocoon. Most people come to nonviolence after having had at least some personal experience with violence. The more dramatic you make that difference for the individual, the greater your character's arc. Gandhi's history is interesting that way.

Institutional violence doesn't always respond to nonviolence, but the individuals involved and the politicians behind it sometimes will. Show your character trying to influence two or more of these, with varying success, like convincing one captain not to attack a village or one politician to confront the party line. See the drama and tragedy of this approach in *Schindler's List* in the interactions between Liam Neeson's Schindler and Ralph Fiennes' Nazi.

Nonviolence can devolve into crazy-making, passive-aggressive behavior: "Oh, that's all right, I'll just sit here and watch you eat," or "Whatever you decide is fine," and then, "Does everyone else really like this?"

The goal of nonviolence is to get the other people to see, understand, and support your point of view and then act accordingly. What happens if you get the former but not the latter. Or vice versa?

CIVIL DISOBEDIENCE

In the same vein but more physically engaged than nonviolence is civil disobedience. You don't take up arms, but you turn the rules-and-tools of the oppressor against them in ways that bring attention to your cause and, hopefully, affect change. This is the *Network* solution, after Paddy Chayefsky's novel and film which feature a disillusioned TV anchorman who starts telling the truth - live on air. This approach kicks in when you're mad as hell and you're not gonna take it any more.

Work stoppages, strikes, blue-flu (when cops call in sick), boycotts, tying up customer service, and email-phone-mail campaigns have sometimes been effective. The trick is to follow the rules — to the word, to the letter — so much so that you bug the heck out of the rule makers by wasting their time and tying up their resources.

A. IN ACTION

Sulky teenagers use civil disobedience against parental authority by pushing the line but not going over it, thus driving parents nuts.

Activist Saul Alinski influenced civil disobedience in the 1960s. One tactic against bank policy was for hundreds of depositors to line up, close their accounts and get cash, go to the end of the same line and open a new account with the same cash. All legal, all time-consuming, and all heck for the bank.

Greenpeace, people who chain themselves to trees, and other nature protectionists for the most part try to stay within the law as they conduct their protests, often with picturesque or sometimes tragic exceptions (the ones who don't make for interesting stories).

Czechoslovakia's 1989 Velvet Revolution and Ukraine's 2004 Orange Revolution accomplished their socio-political goals without violence.

B. IN MEDIA

Office workers use this one well, as in Dilbert cartoons.

Kim Stanley Robinson's *Mars* novels pit colonists in civil disobedience against the multinational corporations trying to control the terra-formed red planet.

Iron Jawed Angels portrays American suffragettes protesting to get the vote for women. *Reds* is about idealistic Americans sometimes using civil disobedience in the cause of Communism.

C. IN YOUR CREATIONS

Inner Drives Center of Motivation – Lower Solar Plexus: individual rights and personal power, & Aspirational Solar Plexus: helping others gain their rights.

Free trade, the IMF and World Bank, war profiteering... how can ordinary people take a stand against some of the global practices without destroying everything? How can they encourage a synthesis of the positive aspects of big business with the good of consumers, producers, and ordinary people?

The payoff for this tactic should have your audience cheering. Build up the frustrations and show your antiestablishment heroines trying two to three other tactics that don't work.

Have resistance from some who think using anything of the establishment's would taint their movement.

A defector from the establishment is often the best source of information. Their conversion provides a dramatic character arc. Or perhaps they're just doing it to spite someone else or set them up for a downfall.

Towards the end, showing one of the protestors getting drawn into the establishment would illustrate the lure of power and why it's hard to sustain effective resistance. Exposure of this traitor to the cause can be a key story point. Cypher in *The Matrix* played this traitor role.

FIGHT FIRE WITH FIRE

When none of the above works, you may just need to physically fight back with whatever you have on hand, as some aspects of the Dark Side simply do not respond to anything but force.

You can sometimes counter impersonal Dark Forces by applying impersonal counterforces. If fields flood every spring, build dams or divert the waters. If there are seasonal fires, burn firebreaks. If predators eat your herds, run off or kill the predators, inject a counter-predator, or move your herds. Counter-predators often end up being more trouble than they're worth, though, as do weapons such as landmines and NBCs (nuclear-biological-chemical).

Sometimes a show of force is enough: aircraft carrier battle groups moved to hot spots, rifles on truck gun racks, police patrols, strutting scowls and clenched fists. A small feisty cat-chick in TVs *Andromeda* challenged a huge alien to guess whether she was really clever or really crazy. He deemed either one really dangerous and left her alone.

Though they can be misused, preemptive strikes can deflect or defeat a possible greater danger. Ideally this tactic means you take up arms to squelch a clear-and-present danger exhibiting both capabilities and intent to harm.

A. IN ACTION

Violent tendencies seem inherent in all humans and most of history is the story of fighting over one thing or another: resources, land, power, women, men, animals, slaves, honor, religion, or the way you fix your hair.

Sometimes opposition to the Dark Side is perpetuated by the Dark Side in order to draw others into battle. In his departure speech, President Dwight D. Eisenhower warned against the military-industrial complex unduly influencing foreign policy. The film *Syriana* and the British TV series *Reilly: Ace of Spies,* both based on reality, illustrate how weapons manufacturers and resource power brokers manipulate and perpetuate conflict around the world in order to keep their businesses flourishing.

B. IN MEDIA

From ancient India to Mesoamerica and all around the world, myths recount pitched battles between the Dark and the Light. *The Lord of the Rings* trilogy raises this concept to multiple hours of impressive battles.

More than just a tactic, many war stories and martial arts movies focus on fighting for fighting's sake.

Some war stories comment on the idiocy of war or the addictions we have to violence: *Paths of Glory, All's Quiet on the Western Front, Johnny Got His Gun, Apocalypse Now, The Battle of Algiers.*

Some display the honor of men and women in battle: *Zulu, Patton, Gunga Din, Khyber Pass, Glory, Starship Troopers, 300.*

Others reveal the games played by great gods or powers, with warriors as pawns: *The Iliad, The Aeneid, Lawrence of Arabia, The Thin Red Line, Babylon 5.*

Spartacus, Magnificent Seven, The Seven Samurai, Red Dawn, El Cid, The Fellowship of the Ring, and *The Last Samurai* feature a few good guys going up against a whole lot of bad guys.

Shane, Rambo, The Highlander, Xena, Batman, Spiderman, Wonder Woman, Sarah Connor in *The Terminator*, and most superheroes stand alone against the Darkness.

The *World of Warcraft* multiplayer online game, *Age of Mythology, Age of Empire, Star Wars*, and all the other battle games engage this tactic of armed confrontation.

C. IN YOUR CREATIONS

Inner Drives Center of Motivation – Lower Solar Plexus: the Warrior center, band of brothers, defense of self, & Root: sheer survival.

Contact the military Public Relations offices for assistance in information, personnel, and equipment for your projects.

Two things to consider about the enemy as your protagonist prepares to encounter them are 1) their capabilities and 2) their intent. No point wasting your own resources in overkill or in fighting the wrong enemy.

War stories offer the opportunity for valor, to sacrifice one's own self for the greater good. It's usually redemptive to have the person who previously wimped out be the one to fall on the grenade.

Just as in any Hero's Journey, be sure your hero finds effective allies and weapons.

To escalate tension, escalate the weapons and danger.

Cut off the head, the rest will die. Or find the center of gravity and tip the enemy off balance.

Tension appears when you assign a mission but not enough resources to accomplish it. Indiana Jones is often in this situation and has to just make it up as he goes along.

YOU SAY YOU WANT A REVOLUTION?

Now that the guns are out, let's talk about other armed approaches to battling badness. Revolutions and coups have been occurring long before Greek god Zeus and his siblings overthrew their father Chronos (*Clash of the Titans*).

The problem with revolutions is that the situations often just revolve like a pig on a spit: it's a different side getting roasted, but it's all the same pig. When successful, revolutions often spawn counterrevolutions and the fighting just goes on and on.

A coup is different from a revolution in that it's usually a small, powerful insider group, usually military, that breaks ranks and tosses out the leadership. Because it's a military force rather than the will of people, as in a revolution, coups often lead to long-standing military dictatorships.

Coups are a favorite tool of empire. Alexander the Great, the Roman Empire, Genghis Khan, European colonizers, and America have all installed friendly rulers in lands they've conquered or wish to exploit in some way. Often called "client governments," a more descriptive term is "puppet regimes."

A. IN ACTION

The American Revolution, French Revolution, Russian Revolution, Spanish Civil War, Simon Bolivar's revolutionary leadership in

South America, China's Communist Revolution, etc., etc., etc.

Lawrence of Arabia was encouraged to encourage Bedouin tribes to rebel against the Turks by promising them land and power. In a betrayal of those promises, the Treaty of Versailles after World War I created new countries (including Iraq) and client governments of nomadic tribes in the Middle East. Many of today's conflicts, though founded in centuries-old enmities, were exacerbated by this oil-driven manipulation.

American-supported coups include Augusto Pinochet in Chile, Ferdinand Marcos in the Philippines, Manuel Noriega in Panama, the overthrow of the democratically elected Mohammed Mossadegh in Iran and his replacement with our guy the Shah Reza Pahlavi, Viet Nam's Ngo Diem, Indonesia's Suharto, Saddam Hussein in Iraq, etc., etc., etc. The early 2000s populist movement in Latin America threatens longtime U.S. hegemony and influence in that region.

B. IN MEDIA

Under Fire, The Mission, Salvador, A Tale of Two Cities, The Scarlet Pimpernel, For Whom the Bell Tolls, Missing, The Year of Living Dangerously.

In *Viva Zapata* Marlon Brando plays a Mexican peasant who leads a revolution and then becomes just like the oppressors.

In *Fight Club,* Edward Norton and his alter ego Brad Pitt foment a violent revolution out of frustration with their passionless, consumer-oriented culture.

Three Kings shows American soldiers involved in the aborted Kurdish coup during Gulf War I.

C. IN YOUR CREATIONS

Inner Drives Center of Motivation - Lower Solar Plexus: polarity, and personal power at the expense of others.

Define the oppressors and show it getting worse. Or are the rebels just feisty power mongerers exaggerating the oppression?

To illustrate the dangers, show an unsuccessful attempt to rebel.

Oppressors are usually conservative and control-oriented. Show their point of view and justified fear of giving in to rebel demands: It would change everything.

Rebels often want a return to the good old days, so show why and how that was lost. Or, they are visionaries who want to move forward. Be sure to define these different approaches so we know the direction of motivation.

Show how the seeds of a revolution's downfall lie in the fact that it fights its opposite and risks becoming that.

CUT TO THE CHASE

Contrary to popular opinion, you *can* run away from your problems — if you run far enough, fast enough, in the right direction. When other tactics have been tried and failed, sometimes running is simply the smartest thing to do.

A. IN ACTION

You can run, but not always hide, as extradition treaties between countries helps control cross-border crime, and Interpol enforces basic laws worldwide, from white-collar crimes to drug and human trafficking.

The United Nations has an entire branch dedicated to refugees. The developed world is currently battling with how best to integrate the flood of mostly Developing World immigrants who've run from bad economic or political situations.

B. IN MEDIA

A good part of every action-adventure movie involves the chase. Three iconic run-for-it films are *Butch Cassidy and the Sundance Kid*, *Thelma and Louise*, and *The Fugitive*.

Though not a chase movie, at the end of *Casablanca*, all the main characters are running away to fight another day.

In the dramatic film *El Norte*, immigrants run from Latin American poverty to troubling lives in LA.

Other run-for-it movies are *Road Warrior*, *Catch Me if You Can*, *Brother Where Art Thou*, and *Apocalypto*.

In games, the "run" button gets a lot of wear.

C. IN YOUR CREATIONS

Inner Drives Center of Motivation – Root: Sheer survival.

Somewhere in the setup let us know who's chasing who and some of why. Some can be saved for later revelation, but unless we get some sympathy for the hero and an understanding of why he's running we simply won't care, no matter how exciting the visuals are.

Because of it's visceral impact, try to save chases as exhilarating punctuation between sequences of character development, or save it for the last-ditch effort after all other tactics have failed.

Use details of the chase as metaphor for what the character's going through. In *The Fugitive* Dr. Richard Kimble leaps off the dam (concrete civilization) into the falls (dangerous unknown Nature). In *Thelma and Louise* the girls speed away from dangerous males (and certain jail time) into yet another unknown freedom from an unwanted past (pretty certain death).

Seek sanctuary

This tactic is usually grasped in chase situations when the heroine or the audience needs a rest, or you need to deliver some information to her or to the audience.

Living out their own metaphor, holy ground usually offers physical sanctuary for anyone, criminals included, along with the opportunity for spiritual salvation. Some deities take up residence in their temples, others just make regular scheduled appearances but are available for 911 calls. Regardless, the presence of a good deity can deter evil.

Public places sometimes provide sanctuary, depending on how worried the villain is about exposure. It may work if a hypocritical public figure is after the heroine, but don't count on it with mindless demons or ravaging beasts.

Cyberspace offers sanctuary too, now that cameras and the Internet can make any place public, as overzealous cops and rude citizens have discovered to their chagrin.

Shifting elements, geography, or dimensions can create sanctuary, like jumping into water to escape a lion (don't try it with tigers — they swim), joining the Witness Protection Program, or the sci-fi trick of hiding in hyperspace.

A. In action

Social services offer discreet homes for abused spouses, mostly women. But there are plenty of men who get physically as well as emotionally and spiritually abused by their domestic partners. Where can they go?

Church leaders around the country protested when proposed U.S. immigration laws threatened to force them to turn in illegals who came for assistance.

A few countries without extradition treaties and with very loose banking laws offer safe haven for tax dodgers and criminals. They tend to be in warm climates with strong umbrella drinks and are favored by murderous military dictators.

Hostage-taking is an attempt to create a sanctuary space.

B. IN MEDIA

In *The Highlander* series and films, churches are off-limits for head removal (guaranteed one per episode), but a lot of decapitating swordfights occur on the front steps of a lot of churches.

In *His Dark Materials* books and film, characters use a magic knife to cut doorways between dimensions and find safety.

Odd that Switzerland, a staunchly neutral country, doesn't have more international conflict refugees; maybe it's just too cold and small.

C. IN YOUR CREATIONS

Inner Drives Center of Motivation – Root: Sheer survival.

One way to use this tool is to establish early on that a certain place offers sanctuary, but make it really difficult to get there or to get in. Like Switzerland?

Another way is to surprise us, e.g. hurtling over the waterfall reveals a hidden cave where your heroes can hide.

If set up by showing how or why sanctuary has worked well before, betrayals of sanctuary can be shocking.

Shift from one aspect of the Dark Side to another for more conflict: Your characters find physical sanctuary but their own Dwellers (claustrophobia, self-destructiveness) betray them, or a Dark Force (earthquake, tsunami) makes it all for naught.

TRIALS, TRUTHS, AND RECONCILIATIONS

Retaliation is an ancient concept easily corrupted into eye-for-an-eye vendettas that ravage people, families, and entire cultures for ages. Restorative justice is based on giving back, not continuing to take away. It's about shining light into the dark places, admitting wrongdoing, and starting fresh. It's what redemptive religions preach but don't always practice. Restitution and reparations make more societal sense because they restore balance and can defuse hatreds.

Many victims just want to be heard and understood, especially if the crimes they suffered were done in silence or secrecy that denied their humanity. Particularly in crimes like ethnic cleansing or genocide, public acknowledgement of a person's right to exist restores dignity for many.

A. IN ACTION

Modern war crimes trials are designed to give victims a voice, to expose previously hidden atrocities, and to design social systems that compensate victims and prevent the problem from recurring.

In the 1990s, South Africa's Truth and Reconciliation Committee (TRC) gave both victims and perpetrators of apartheid injustices the opportunity to be heard in open court and to request amnesty.

Augusto Pinochet of Chile, the Somozas of Nicaragua, and Ferdinand Marcos of the Philippines all perpetrated crimes against their own people while Western governments turned a blind eye. It's still going on in Burma and other developing nations. Even when dictators fall and are brought to trial, as Marcos was, most countries never recover their stolen riches.

There was a lot of grumbling about the speedy hanging of Saddam Hussein before more of his victims' relatives had their say and before all those individuals, businesses, and governments complicit in his actions could be exposed.

B. IN MEDIA

The 1961 Stanley Kramer film *Judgment at Nuremburg* is a moving courtroom drama about Nazi war criminals.

The movies *Red Dust* and *In My Country* center around South Africa's TRC.

We could use more stories in support of this concept.

C. IN YOUR CREATIONS

Inner Drives Centers of Motivation – Aspirational Solar Plexus: concern for the greater good, & Throat: law and justice.

Show the contrast between how a person was treated before and after the recognition of the trial: from beaten-down to upright, from furtive to firm, from mute to speaking out.

The scariest thing about these situations is how far the Dark Side reaches. Exposing good guys who let the bad guys get away with it can create dramatic surprises.

Courtroom dramas must be tightly written and very well executed. Hopefully we'll see more good ones as we get more fallout from the Cold War and current events. The new International Criminal Court can only try crimes committed after 2002, but it would be a good setting for an international suspense film.

Not everyone agrees in forgive and forget. Some say you needn't forgive others for doing evil, but you don't want to stay stuck in your own hatred. Others say they can forgive, but they'll never forget. These inner conflicts offer good dramatic challenges.

THE PRIMROSE PATH

Though more common in the past, a Don Juan or a Temptress might be tamed via seduction into marital bliss, as the promise of true love lures them from pirate ship to pipe-and-slippers or cook-ing-and-cradles. Often seen as taming our wilder nature, marriage and parenthood supposedly make the self-centered individual a better cog in society's machine.

Part of this is simple physics: you can't penetrate something without being simultaneously surrounded by it. While seducers are usually the stronger personality in a couple, the mere fact of them engaging in "normal" situations, often under societal pressure, can alter the dynamics and defuse this sometimes harmful, seductive Dweller.

A. IN ACTION

Science now proves a common observation: females choose to sex-mate with rugged alpha males and to home-make with softer, nurturing males. Yet more American women live alone now than ever before (51%), many by choice. Most divorces are instigated by women. More people are cohabitating, and more children are born out of wedlock every year.

Though marriage is apparently losing its allure, a huge industry revolves around advising women how to find their soul mate, get them to commit, and once committed, how to plan the perfect wedding.

Jokes abound about the wife as ball-and-chain, yet studies show married men are healthier and happier than single men. It's the opposite for women.

B. IN MEDIA

Fairy tales and romances typically end at the wedding: the chase is over, the lovers are united, the tension is released — no more drama. Think how the sexual tension in these TV series fizzled once the couples finally got together: Maddie and David in *Moonlighting*, Niles and Daphne in *Frasier*, and Mulder and Scully in *The X Files*.

Doris Day/Rock Hudson movies of the '50s and '60s and the 2003 paean to them, *Down With Love*, humorously follow this Primrose Path pattern as the flawed Don Juan is trapped and transformed into perfect hubby material.

Domestication failed with Rhett Butler in *Gone with the Wind* and Alexandria Ripley's sequel novel, *Scarlett*. Classics *Hedda Gabler*, *Madame Bovary*, *A Doll's House*, and *Anna Karenina* also deal with dissatisfaction in domesticity.

Often it's the man who rescues the woman into the protection of domesticity with varying degrees of success, like in the movies *Pretty Woman*, where businessman Richard Gere rescues prostitute Julia Roberts, and *Blue Sky*, where military man Tommy Lee Jones saves his wild troubled wife, Jessica Lange.

C. IN YOUR CREATIONS

Inner Drives Center of Motivation – Sacral (sex-fear-money) moving to Lower Solar Plexus (pair bonding)or Aspirational Solar Plexus (family inclusiveness). See the chapters "Peter Pans, Papas, and Pygmalions" and "Marilyns, Moms, and Muses" in *Inner Drives*.

Select a couple of selfish behaviors that pair-bonding will transform: me-actions to we-actions; sexual promiscuity to exclusivity; bachelor housekeeping to Martha Stewart housekeeping.

Show a woman torn between alpha and beta males and how she chooses one or juggles both.

On the negative side, show how bonding can devolve into bondage, usually emotional, sometimes actual.

Explore situations were marriages are arranged but fail to transform the individual, such as in Deepa Mehta's films *Water* and *Fire*.

Contrary to most evidence, the myth still exists that true love and marriage are the end-all, be-all goal. Explore the positive and negatives of this.

THE ROAD TO DAMASCUS

The tools of conversion are emotional and appeal to that spark of the Light said to be within all creatures, just waiting to be ignited by recognition and redemption.

The early 2000s saw an increase in spiritually slanted stories, from the Christian-based *Left Behind* series to the New Age *What The Bleep Do We Know?* and many in between. A common flaw in "spiritual" stories is that they are spineless, illogical, or trite. A writer's belief in the omniscience and omnipotence of any deity or system can make it difficult to create realistic opposition and hence, dramatic conflict.

Since you can't reason with or appeal to the Dark Forces such as gravity or time, conversion only works for Dwellers on the Threshold and the Dark Brotherhood.

A. IN ACTION

Some religions are based on their founder's conversion from a regular, or sometimes debauched, life to one of austerities and holiness: Buddha, Mohammed, Mormon's Joseph Smith, and most charismatic sects.

Twelve-step programs offer support for conversions from self-destructive Dweller behavior. There's a joke that even compulsive talkers have a group, On-and-on Anon.

Conversions, particularly religious ones, use emotional appeals and dissuade logical thinking. People are told to think less and feel more.

Though seeing the light and changing the heart can defuse the Dark Side and bring about many positive changes, there's a Dark Side to conversions too — those forced under torture like the Spanish Inquisition, and deadly cults like those of Charles Manson, Jim Jones, and Japan's Aum Shinrikyo.

B. IN MEDIA

In the Bible's New Testament, the Jew Saul was headed to Damascus to persecute Christians when he was blinded by a bright light and heard the voice of Jesus. Converting to Christianity, he became the influential Saint Paul.

Arthurian legends about the Holy Grail are said to symbolize our heart's search for spiritual truth and nourishment. The very search ennobles one, and sight of the Grail brings transformation.

Stories where characters either undergo a change of heart or have already done so and now have their faith tested are *A History of Violence*, Clint Eastwood's *Unforgiven*, and Samuel L. Jackson in *Pulp Fiction*. Jeff Bridges finds self forgiveness in *The Fisher King*. Through the five years of the *Babylon 5* series, G'Kar goes from a hostile freed-slave warrior-ambassador to a revered spiritual leader teaching peace. The *Buffy the Vampire Slayer* TV series has some forced conversions for vampires Spike and Angel. But they don't hold, and that's good drama.

C. IN YOUR CREATIONS

Inner Drives Center of Motivation – regardless of where they begin, the end result is Aspirational Solar Plexus, sometimes Heart.

If you are a true believer, keep in mind that many others are not or that they truly believe something quite different from you. To reach others with your message, however powerful it is to you, your story must still fulfill the classic requirements of effective storytelling, including a worthy opponent, appropriate danger, and satisfactory realistic resolution (not a *deus ex machina*).

Archetypes and universal truths of most spiritual systems are similar in concept but different in execution. Approach with the familiar (the Golden Rule), and then offer the unique (Buddhism's Eightfold Path).

Conversions are like revolutions — everything contains its opposite. Show how a character's excesses in one area (sex, drinking, violence) convert into denial (chastity, abstinence, pacifism).

The epiphany of conversion is often a turning point in stories, when a character suddenly sees the light and begins helping those she spurned or took advantage of before. Show the reasons why she didn't help before, and give a solid emotional reason for her conversion. Somebody usually then says, "I was wrong about you," as she pitches in to save the day.

Spiritual conversions draw one upward in aspiration and outward in service. Show a self sacrifice for the greater good, either with reluctance or rapture.

A conversion initially brings dramatic change, but that wears off pretty quickly. Show the dangers of doubt, temptation, and reversion.

GET A SENSE OF PERSPECTIVE

Some people claim to know the precise nature of good and evil. Others who have dared to look with open mind and heart claim it is an unfathomable mystery. Much of the mystery is a matter of perspective and scale.

The little swat on the bottom hurts the toddler's feelings, if not her diaper-padded bottom, but it keeps her away from the dangers of the open street and open flame. Grueling drills and debasements explode the ego and exhaust the body of the new soldier, but instill lifesaving skills. One broken heart pours forth poetry to comfort and inspire myriad other yearning hearts. A conquered people assimilates the invaders and a stronger, more vibrant culture results.

Without getting sappy about making lemonade out of lemons, a determination to find positive value in any situation goes a long way to defusing the power of a negative situation. Also, life is constant change, so what was good one day is bad the next, and vice versa. Perspective determines motivation and justification for actions. Shift perspective and you may well shift actions.

A. IN ACTION

Historical research and archaeological discoveries shift perspective on Judaism and Christianity. The apocryphal books of the Bible, the Dead Sea Scrolls, and the new Judas Gospel reveal dramatically different versions of the holy canons. *Holy Blood Holy Grail, Woman with the Alabaster Jar,* and *The Da Vinci Code* popularized different perspectives on Jesus, Mary Magdalene, and official Christianity.

The earth used to be flat and the center of the universe. Bleeding and maggots were once in favor but were later seen as barbaric medical practices; they're both now back "in." Slavery and child labor were once business-as-usual in Western countries; they still are in many other parts of the world. Germany, Japan, and Italy were the Axis of Evil in World War II.

B. IN MEDIA

In *The Hitchhiker's Guide to the Galaxy* zany, arrogant Zaphod Beeblebrox is put into an Infinite Perspective Device and forced to eat Fairy Cake that holographically illustrates one's infinitesimal insignificance in the universe. Most people go mad, but Zaphod, the center of *his* universe, is unfazed.

A defeated fighter in the TV series *Babylon 5* wryly observes that if life were fair, then every bad thing that happened to him would be his fault, so he finds solace in the general hostility of an indifferent universe.

The Tarot card of The Wheel of Fortune (Key 10) shows the ups and downs of Fate. Frank Sinatra's song "That's Life" puts it in lyrics.

The endings of both *Men in Black* movies show nested universes, with our own just a tiny marble in some other's game. Monty Python's "Galaxy Song" is a clever rendition of this concept and you can view the visuals on the Internet.

Tom Cruise's selfish character in *Rainman* changes when his perspective about his brother shifts. Children who increase their self esteem also shift their levels of accomplishment, as in *Stand and Deliver* and *Freedom Writers*.

As we become more aware of the consequences of our indulgences, virtues morph to vices. Cigarette smoking was sexy when Marlene Dietrich or Cary Grant did it, but by 1999 cigarette industries were the bad guys in *The Insider*. Drinking was sophisticated in *The Thin Man* series and stupid fun in *Animal House*. The 1981 comedy hit *Arthur* showed indulgence of the happy drunk, but in 1995 *Leaving Las Vegas* showed a tragic drunk sliding down to death.

C. IN YOUR CREATIONS

Inner Drives Center of Motivation – Ajna: a sense of time, proportion, balance, and integration.

For Dweller problems, often just learning that other people have similar problems can offer relief from feeling like you're being selectively punished. Group therapy sessions aim for this.

Showing how trivial or common they truly are can often deflate the self-important antagonist.

Taking a character through shifts from 1) a tribal (instinctual, restrictive) perspective to 2) individual (selfish) perspective to 3) a global (inclusive, generous) perspective can provide dramatic character arcs.

Telling stories from an atypical perspective can shake up consensus reality, as did *Little Big Man* about cowboys and Indians, *My Life as a Dog* about a child's experiences, and *Wicked: The Life and Times of the Wicked Witch of the West* about the Oz story. Make your characters eat the Fairy Cake and see reality from a totally different perspective.

CONCLUSION

From these ways to battle the badness, and more that may come to your mind, you can select an appropriate approach for your protagonist-versus-antagonist conflict.

Since your story will contain at least two levels of the Dark Side, you can have at least two approaches, one for the personal Dweller and one for the Dark Forces, or the Dark Brotherhood. In longer forms such as novels or TV series you can go through more approaches; in features you'll do best to concentrate on just a few, using variations within them and/or ratcheting up the intensity of an approach.

Sometimes the good does not win, but confronting the Dark Side can make your heroes stronger. The cynic snipes, "Stronger for what?" The fan delights in the prospect of a sequel.

∼VI∾

WORKING WITH THE DARK SIDE

Previous sections have explored content; now let's look at how you can present that content in effective ways. Here you'll find categories for opponents, the progression from annoyance to annihilation, and some thoughts about future challenges. As storytellers, it's your privilege, honor, and duty to help us all imagine what we may face in the future and to help prepare us for it. ∼

13.
STORY TOOLS

✦ Selecting your hero's worthy opponent

✦ The sliding scale

✦ The Dark Side of our future

SELECTING THE WORTHY OPPONENT

A conflict between Bambi and Godzilla would not last very long, and there's no doubt about the outcome. To engage our attention you need to give your protagonist a worthy opponent. Most stories are better for a buildup in conflict, a progression of challenges, and a correspondence of inner and outer resistance.

Select your conflicts from these categories and intertwine two or three of them for more depth and meaning:

> Self – the Dwellers on the Threshold. Building skills, over-coming phobias, strengthening weaknesses. *Karate Kid, Rocky, Shine, The Piano, The Man Who Would Be King, Leaving Las Vegas, The Unforgiven, Adaptation, Sideways.*

> Lovers & rivals – Conflict is ready-made in this category. Screwball comedies pit lovers against each other. *Adam's Rib, Bringing Up Baby, The Philadelphia Story, When Harry Met Sally.* Romantic comedies and dramas often revolve around love triangles: *Camelot, Double Indemnity, Sunset Boulevard, Body Heat, Indecent Proposal, Basic Instinct, No Way Out, A Streetcar Named Desire, The Graduate, Death Becomes Her, My Best Friend's Wedding, The Wedding Crashers.*

Other individuals – they're out to get your heroine or are just plain obstructive or evil. *The Odd Couple, High Noon, Grumpy Old Men, The Player, Heathers, The Big Lebowski, Cape Fear, Patriot Games, Face/Off, The Italian Job.*

Family – they hold him back, make unreasonable demands, are unavailable or abusive, emotionally or physically. *Romeo and Juliet, Hamlet, Ordinary People, Muriel's Wedding, Once Were Warriors, Secrets of the Ya-Ya Sisterhood, Finding Nemo, The Lion King, Postcards from the Edge, The Incredibles.*

Profession – challenges her, makes demands that compromise her integrity, put her in danger. *Wall Street, Under Fire, Working Girl, Nine to Five, The Long Kiss Goodnight, Rocky, Office Space, Training Day, The Constant Gardener, Good Night and Good Luck, Syriana, World Trade Center.*

Society – restricts or represses personal expression, unfairly punishes individuality. *A Clockwork Orange, Sense and Sensibility, Pride and Prejudice, Bride and Prejudice, Evita, My Beautiful Laundrette, Down and Out in Beverly Hills, In and Out.*

Politics & Bureaucracies – rage against the machine. *Metropolis, Three Days of the Condor, All the President's Men, Being There, Dave, The West Wing, The Manchurian Candidate, Brazil, 1984, Brave New World, Becket, The Lion in Winter,* and most spy stories.

Religion – crisis of faith, repression, persecution, religious wars. *Queen Margot, Witness, The Last Temptation of Christ, Dangerous Beauty, Luther, The Mission, The Scarlet Letter, Agnes of God, Water, Earth, Kingdom of God, The Da Vinci Code.*

Environment – the Dark Forces. *The Grapes of Wrath, Jaws, Waterworld, Twister, Outbreak, The Ghost and the Darkness, The Right Stuff, The Perfect Storm, Backdraft, The Day After Tomorrow, Armageddon.*

Technology – run awry. *Frankenstein(s), Dr. Jekyll and Mr. Hyde, The Andromeda Strain, WarGames, A.I., Terminator, The Matrix, Blade Runner, I, Robot, Jurassic Park, Battlestar Gallactica, Minority Report.*

Wars - and warring factions. *Henry V, Lawrence of Arabia, Godfather, Gangs of New York, Apocalypse Now, Under Siege, The Thin Red Line, Platoon,* most war movies.

Gods, monsters, magic, demons, and aliens – *Them, It, Invasion of the Body Snatchers, The Thing, Close Encounters of the Third Kind, Alien, Independence Day, Signs, The Mummy, Buffy the Vampire Slayer, Charmed,* most horror movies.

The Dark Brotherhood – the really big bad guys. *The Seventh Seal, Black Orpheus, Babylon 5, Conspiracy Theory, Eyes Wide Shut, Legend, The Lord of the Rings.*

THE SLIDING SCALE

When you need to up the stakes, go up the sliding scale. Like a thermometer that indicates rising temperatures, or a gauge that measures RPMs, this can be a measure of how it all starts out rather innocently and then gets progressively worse. Here's just a small sample of naughty-to-bad-to-evil:

- mentally criticizing someone's fashion sense, or lack thereof
- making catty remarks about them to someone else
- making catty remarks to the fashion victim herself
- taking the bigger slice of cake
- hiding the cake so no one else gets any
- denying education, medical care
- denial of civil rights
- unfair incarceration
- verbal/emotional violence

- physical violence
- rape
- torture
- murder
- serial murders
- ethnic cleansing
- genocide
- setting off plagues and weapons of mass destruction
- ecologically destroying continents, and planets
- blowing up planets
- blowing up the cosmos

Add your own, rearrange the items... just let us know what actions your characters actually think are worse, or if they aren't conscious of being bad, let us know what the system they exist in considers worse, and explore their motivations and ramifications.

THE DARK SIDE OF OUR FUTURE

Okay, you blew up the Death Star, but wasn't that an escape pod tumbling off into the distance? Count on it, there will be another challenge, and another, and another.

The tools of conflict progress from sticks and rocks to nuclear bombs to... what's next? As science and technology leap ahead of philosophy and psychology, what new Powers of Darkness will we face? As storytellers, your duty and your privilege is to help discern that and to give us the insights and inspirations to deal with it.

Select two or three problems from these different categories and nest them like those little painted Russian dolls, so that your story progressively reveals deeper interconnected conflicts.

PERSONAL PROBLEMS

techno-phobia
alienation
isolation
compassion fatigue
future shock
regression to fundamentalism as protection from modernism
physical mutations, allergies, and illnesses
inability to focus and learn (too-short attention spans)

SOCIETAL PROBLEMS

failed safety nets of medicine, education, elder care
personal responsibility vs. social programs
emergency preparedness - floods, epidemics, storms
migrations, refugees
apocalyptic fracturing into isolated communes or compounds
integration vs. assimilation for immigrants and invaders
education/training for citizenship, creativity, and workforce
censorship, freedom of press, brainwashing, dumbing down
despotism, anarchy, police states
depressions, recessions, market crashes

BELIEF PROBLEMS

gods and religions vs. other gods and other religions
secularism vs. religionists
neo-social Darwinism – survival of the fittest
aliens (plus alien implants, subversion, manipulation)
cults
fundamentalism
superstition
cynicism devolving into debasement, treachery, and chaos

TECHNOLOGY PROBLEMS

metal fatigue and metal shortages (already happening)

nano-bots and implants gone bad

cloning gone bad

genetically engineered food gone bad

genetically engineered animals and people gone bad

biological-chemical warfare

nuclear proliferation

war in space with fallout on earth

computer-electronics failure

satellite failure

NATURE AND ENVIRONMENTAL PROBLEMS

animals gain self consciousness and demand equal rights

the plant or mineral kingdoms advance to ???? (you tell us)

pollution

habitat destruction

extinctions

climate change

water wars (considered the next big resource problem)

rising sea levels – mass migrations

asteroids striking earth

polar shifts

cosmic rays

UNKNOWN PROBLEMS

extraterrestrials: hostile, or friendly but still dangerous

proof of ancient highly advanced civilizations here on earth

proof of ancient civilizations on other planets

proof of current civilizations on other planets

proof of underground civilizations (extinct or extant)

genetic mutations via natural selection

You tell us!

CONCLUSION

Using these three conceptual mechanisms in your stories you can select appropriate antagonists, plot rising conflict, and challenge our imaginations. As in any creative endeavor, strive for both familiarity and surprise, for elegance and improbability, for reassurance and challenge. When you succeed in this, your work will sparkle with a Light guaranteed to both attract and, somewhat at least, transform the Dark Side.

CONCLUSION

Throughout this book we've explored many aspects of the Dark Side. We have become acquainted with various villains, seen how they got that way, and how they operate. We've also explored ways your characters can counter the Dark Side and ways to use these concepts in your stories.

Hopefully this book will inspire you to explore further, to hold our human fears up to the Light, to reveal our Dark Sides, and to test our strengths and weaknesses. Storytellers can also show us what we ourselves might become if we do not consciously craft the resolutions of our own lives in alignment with the passion and the peace we all long for.

Storytellers are like the Holy Grail knight Parsifal. Unlike pure Galahad who sees the Light and is taken up into it, and unlike bad-boy Gawain who cannot see the Light at all, Parsifal stands in the-place-between. He sees the Light, but he remains in the world to serve the Grail. Parsifal becomes the bridge and the doorway for others who cannot yet see the Light but who can see him.

Your stories can be both bridge and doorway for others. Use the information in this book to bring your own Light to the Power of the Dark Side, then transmute it into inspiration and entertainment for us all.

Onward and Upward!

BIBLIOGRAPHY

Alighieri, Dante. *The Divine Comedy*. New York: Penguin Classics, 2003.

Armstrong, Karen. *The Battle for God*. New York: Ballantine Books, 2001.
— also see her many other books on religions.

Bailey, Alice. *Esoteric Psychology I*. New York: Lucis Publishing Company, 1936.
— *Esoteric Psychology II*. New York: Lucis Publishing Company, 1942.

Bettelheim, Bruno. *The Uses of Enchantment*. New York: Random House, 1977.

Blavatsky, Madame Helena P. *The Secret Doctrine: The Synthesis of Science, Religion, and Philisophy*. Pasadena, CA: Theosophical University Press, 1999.

Brown, Norman O. *Life Against Death: The Psychoanalytical Meaning of History*. Middleton, CT: Wesleyan University News, 1985.

Budge, E. A. Wallis. *The Egyptian Book of the Dead*. New York: Dover Publications, Inc., 1967.

Bulfinch, Thomas. *Bulfinch's Mythology*. New York: Random House, 1998.

Campbell, Joseph. *The Flight of the Wild Gander*. New York: HarperCollins. 1990.
—. *The Hero With a Thousand Faces*. Princeton: Princeton University Press, 1972.
—. *The Inner Reaches of Outer Space*. New York: Harper & Row, 1986.
—. *The Masks of God*. New York: Penguin Books, 1964.
—. *The Power of Myth*. New York: Doubleday, 1988.
—. *Transformation of Myth Through Time*. New York: Harper Perennial, 1990.

Cavendish, Richard. *Legends of the World.* New York: Barnes & Noble Books, 1994.

Conrad, Joseph. *The Heart of Darkness.* London: Hesperus Press, 2003.

Cumont, Franz. *The Mysteries of Mithra.* New York: Dover Publications, Inc. 1956.

Dawkins, Richard. *The God Delusion.* New York: Bantam Press, 2006.

Dawkins, Richard. *A Devil's Chaplain: Reflections on Hope, Lies, Science, and Love.* New York: Mariner Books, 2004.
— *The God Delusion.* New York: Bantam Press, 2006.
— *The Selfish Gene.* London: Oxford University Press, USA, 2006.

Dennett, Daniel. *Breaking the Spell: Religion as a Natural Phenomenon.* New York: Penguin, 2007.

Dobbs, Michael. *House of Cards.* New York: Harper Collins, 1990.

Durant, Will and Ariel Durant. *The Lessons of History.* MJF Books, 1997.
—. *The Story of Civilization, Volumes I-XI.* New York: Simon and Schuster, 1966.
—. *The Story of Philosophy.* New York: Pocket, 1991.

Easwaran, Eknath. *The Bhagavad Gita for Daily Living.* Petaluma, CA: Nilgiri Press, 1979.

Eisler, Riane. *The Chalice and the Blade: Our History, Our Future.* Gloucester, MA: Peter Smith Publisher, 1994.

Evans-Wentz, W. Y. *The Tibetan Book of the Dead.* New York: Oxford University Press, 1960.

Fischer, David H. *Historians' Fallacies: Toward a Logic of Historical Thought.* New York: Harper Perennial, 1970.

Fitzgerald, Edward. *Rubaiyat of Omar Khayyam.* New York: Random House, 1947.

Frazer, Sir James. *The Golden Bough: A Study in Magic and Religion.* New York: Palgrave MacMillan, 2003. [Multi-volume, 5614 pp. also available in smaller editions]

Fromm, Erich. *The Anatomy of Human Destructiveness.* New York: Owl Books, 1994.
—. *Escape from Freedom.* Owl Books, 1994.

Froud, Brian and Alan Lee. *Faeries.* London: Pavilion Books, 2002.

Gibbs, Laura, trans. *Aesop's Fables.* New York: Oxford University Press, 2002.

Godwin, Malcolm. *Angels: An Endangered Species.* New York: Simon & Schuster, 1990.

Goodrich, Norma Lorre. *Guinevere.* New York: Harper Perennial, 1992.
—. *Heroines: DemiGoddess, Prima Donna, Movie Star.* New York: Harper Perennial, 1994.
—. *King Arthur.* New York: Harper Perennial, 1989.
—. *Merlin.* New York: Harper Perennial, 1989.

Grant, Joan. *Winged Pharoah.* York, South Africa: Ariel Press, 1986.

Graves, Robert. *I, Claudius.* New York: Vintage, 1989.
—. *Claudius, The God.* New York: Vintage, 1989.
—. *The White Goddess.* New York: Faber and Faber, 1939.

Hall, Manly P. *Secret Teachings of All Ages.* Los Angeles, CA: The Philosophical Society, Inc., 1928.

Hamilton, Edith. *Mythology: Timeless Tales of Gods and Heroes.* New York: Warner Books, Inc., 1999.

Harvey, Jerry. *The Abilene Paradox and other Meditations on Management.* San Francisco: Jossey-Bass, 1996.

Hauser, Mark. *Moral Minds: How Nature Designed Our Universal Sense of Right and Wrong.* New York: Ecco, 2006.

Hedges, Chris. *War is a Force Which Gives Us Meaning*. New York: Anchor, 2003.

Holy Bible. New King James Version. Nashville, TN: Thomas Nelson, Inc., 1989.

Hulsman, John and Anatol Lieven. *Ethical Realism: A Vision for America's Role in the World*. New York: Pantheon, 2006.

Janis, Irving L. *Psychological Studies of Policy Decisions and Fiascoes*. New York: Houghton Mifflin Company, 1982.

Jaynes, Julian. *The Origin of Consciousness in the Breakdown of the Bicameral Mind*. New York: Houghton Mifflin Company, 1976.

John of the Cross, Saint. *The Dark Night of the Soul*. New York: Dover Publications, 2003.

Johnson, Robert A. *Owning Your Own Shadow: Understanding the Dark Side of the Psyche*. San Francisco: Harper San Francisco, 1993.

Johnson, Steven. *Mind Wide Open: Your Brain and the Neuroscience of Everyday Life*. New York: Scribner, 2004.

Keegan, John. *The Mask of Command*. New York: Penguin, 1988.

Kelly, Henry Anscar. *Satan, A Biography*. London: Cambridge University Press, 2007.

Kelly, Sean and Rosemary Rogers. *Saints Preserve Us!: Every Thing You Need to Know About Every Saint You'll Ever Need*. New York: Random House, 1993.

Kirsch, Jonathan. *God Against the Gods: The History of the War Between Monotheism and Polytheism*. New York: Penguin, 2005.
— *The Harlot by the Side of the Road*. New York: Ballantine Books, 1998.

Maguire, Gregory. *Wicked: The Life and Times of the Wicked Witch of the West.* New York: Regan Books, 2004.

Mahabharata, The. Columbia College, auth., Narasimhan, C. V., ed., trans. New York: Columbia University Press, 1997.

Mann, W. Edward. *Orgone, Reich, and Eros: Wilhelm Reich's Theory of Life Energy.* New York: Touchstone Press, 1974.

Mijares, Sharon G., Aliaa Rafia, Rachel Falik, Jenna Eda Schiper. *The Root of All Evil: An Exposition of Prejudice, Fundamentalism and Gender Imbalance.* London: Imprint Academic, 2007.

Miles, Jack. *Christ, a Crisis in the Life of God.* New York: Vintage, 2002.
—. *God, a Biography.* New York: Vintage, 1996.
—. *A History of God: The 4,000 Year Quest of Judaism, Christianity and Islam.* New York: Ballantine Books, 1994.

Miller, Jr., Walter M. *A Canticle for Leibowitz.* New York: Eos, 2006.

Milton, John and John Leonard. *Paradise Lost.* New York: Penguin Classics, 2003.

Neville, Katherine. *The Eight.* London: Corgi Adult, 2006.

New Larousse Encyclopedia of Mythology. New York: Prometheus Press, 1972.

Norretranders, Tor. *The User Illusion.* New York: Viking Penguin, 1998.

Pauwels, Louis and Jacques Bergier. *Morning of the Magicians.* London: Souvenir Press, Ltd., 2001.

Pickover, Clifford A. *Sex, Drugs, Einstein and Elves: Sushi, Psychedelics, Parallel Universes, and the Quest for Transcendence.* Petaluna, CA: Smart Publications, 2005.

Pratchett, Terry and Neil Gaiman. *Good Omens.* New York: HarperTorch, 2006.

Pullman, Philip. *His Dark Materials Trilogy*. New York: Laurel Leaf, 2003.

Qur'an Translation, The. Rawzy, Sayed A. A., ed., Ali, Abdullah Yusuf, trans. Elmhurst, NY: Tahrike Tarsile Qur'an, 1999.

Regardie, Israel. *Ceremonial Magic*. New York: Aquarian Press, 1980.
— *Golden Dawn*. Woodbury, MN: Llewellyn Publications, 2002.

Reich, Wilhelm. *The Function of the Orgasm: Discovery of the Orgone*. New York: Farrar, Strauss and Giroux, 1986.
—. *The Sexual Revolution: Toward a Self-Governing Character Structure*. New York: Farrar, Strauss and Giroux, 1991.

Rig Veda, The. Doniger, Wendy, ed., trans. New York: Penguin Classics, 2005.

Samenow, Stanton. *Inside the Criminal Mind*. New York: Crown, 2004.

Shattuck, Roger. *Forbidden Knowledge: From Prometheus to Pornography*. New York: St. Martin's Press, 1996.

Shermer, Michael. *The Science of Good and Evil*. New York: Owl Books, 2004.
—. *Why People Believe Weird Things: Pseudoscience, Superstition, and Other Confusions of Our Time*. Owl Books, 2002.

Shlain, Leonard. *The Alphabet Versus the Goddess: The Conflict Between Word and Image*. New York: Penguin Group, 1998.

Sitchen, Zecharia. *The Earth Chronicles*. New York: Harper, 1999.

Slater, Philip. *The Pursuit of Loneliness*. New York: Beacon Press, 1990.

Smith, Pamela Jaye. *INNER DRIVES: How to Write and Create Characters Using the Eight Classic Centers of Motivation*. Studio City, CA: Michael Wiese Productions, 2005.

Stephenson, Bret. *From Boys to Men: Spiritual Rites of Passage in an Indulgent Age*. South Paris, ME: Park Street Press, 2006.

Stephenson, Neal. *The Baroque Cycle*. New York: Harper Perennial, 2004.
—. *Cryptonomicron*. New York: Avon, 2002.
—. *Snow Crash*. New York: Spectra, 2000.

Tancredi, Lawrence. *Hardwired Behavior: What Neuroscience Reveals About Morality*. London: Cambridge University Press, 2005.

Turner, Alice K. *The History of Hell*. New York: Harvest Books, 1995.

Voltaire. *Candide:or Optimism* [1759]. New York: Penguin Classics, 1950.

von Gerlach, Geffrey. *Ghost Points*. Phoenix: Rexad Press/Xlibris, 2004.

Waters, Frank. *The Book of the Hopi*. New York: Ballantine Books, 1978.

Wilde, Oscar. *The Complete Fairy Tales of Oscar Wilde*. Winnetka, CA: Norilana Books,2007.

Zimbardo, Phillip. *Lucifer Effect: Understanding How Good People Turn Evil*. New York: Random House, 2007.

Zweig, Connie and Steve Wolf. *Meeting the Shadow*. New York: Tarcher, 1991.
—. *Romancing the Shadow*. New York: Wellspring/Ballantine, 1999.

WEBSITES

Birth2Work – full community education *www.birth2work.org*
Carter Center *www.cartercenter.org*
Center for Enhanced Performance,
    U.S. Army Academy, West Point *www.dean.usma.edu/CEP/*
DARPA: Defense Advanced Research Projects Agency *www.darpa.mil/*
Joseph Campbell Foundation *www.jcf.org*
Institute of Noetic Sciences *www.noetic.org*
Lucifer Effect *www.lucifereffect.com*
Maps of Wars *www.mapsofwar.com/images/Religion.swf*
Massachusetts Institute of Technology's Media Lab *www.media.mit.edu/*

Mindship   *www.mindship.org*
MYTHWORKS   *www.mythworks.net*
Philosophical Research Society   *www.prs.org*
Theosophical Society   *www.theosophical.org/index.html*
Science Week   *www.sciencenews.org*
Scientific American magazine   *www.sciam.com*
Skeptic Magazine   *www.skepticmagazine.org*
Silver Braid Survivors of Sexual Exploitation
      Network   *www.thesilverbraid.org*
Stratfor – Global Intelligence   *www.stratfor.com*

GLOSSARY OF TERMS

Ageless Wisdom - universal insights and information that show up in most cultures' mythologies and spiritual systems. Often attributed to the gods, ancient civilizations, or simply wise humans, the Ageless Wisdom offers advice and disciplines on personal enlightenment and ethics, social systems, planetary and species history, and prophecies. Though the truths are evident in various writings and oral traditions, there is no rigid structure or dogma. If there is any dogma at all, it is not to form dogmas.

agnostic - thinks our human consciousness is unable to know for certain anything about any deities, so keeps an open but skeptical mind.

archetype - a personification of a psychological aspect said accessible to all humans via the collective unconscious. Most mythologies have slightly different versions of the same archetypes: warrior, lover, trickster, mother, etc.

astral plane – emotional realm shared by humanity which is how feelings can be communicated and understood by others. Other planes are the physical, mental, and spiritual. Many traditions say the astral planes are inhabited by all sorts of creatures, some helpful and some not.

atheist - does not believe in the existence of any deity.

Centers of Motivation - the chakras: physiological, psychological, and philosophical Centers that affect and effect our bodies, emotions, and thinking. See my INNER DRIVES book.

chakras - See Centers of Motivation.

dharma - duty, the law, everyday responsibilities. Social, familial, and professional harmony and virtue.

deus ex machina – in a story, supernatural intervention to save the day, usually clumsily done. From old theater where the god (*deus*) was flown or wheeled in via a machine (*ex machina*).

esoteric - hidden, open only to tested and approved initiates; opposite of exoteric, which means out in the open and available to anyone.

Karma - the Hindu version of the law of cause and effect. Often analogous to Isaac Newton's third law: For every action there is an opposite and equal reaction. Karma (both positive and negative) is said to collect and be paid out over many lifetimes. Think of it as a character's "ghost," big time.

Law of Grace - enlightenment, being "born again," baptism, forgiveness... all are examples of this Law in action. Once you get the point of life, existence, and the consequences of your actions, then supposedly you don't need to pay back the debts, since it was all about getting you to become conscious and then stop creating Karma.

Law of Karma - cause and effect. You reap what you sow, positive and or negative, now or in another lifetime.

maya – Sanskrit word meaning "illusion." Hindus and Buddhists see the world of the senses as *maya*, arising from the mind's interpretations of sense perceptions, rather like the imposed reality in *The Matrix* films.

metaphysics - the study of first principals of reality; abstract reasoning; the origins of the world and how it works. Modern physics, astrophysics, and paleology are technically "proving" many things formerly considered "above physics," or metaphysical.

Mithra(s) - ancient Persian god of Light and Truth. A popular god with the Roman Army, the Mithraic religion had seven levels of initiation. Many of the teachings migrated over to Christianity.

Mystery Schools - teach the Ageless Wisdom, the Physics of Metaphysics: how things, people, and systems really work; the nature of reality; the nature of consciousness and the unconscious; the interdependency and reciprocal workings of the soul-mind-brain-body connections. Modern physics, astrophysics, and paleology are technically "proving" many things these Schools have always taught. There is no structure, no bureaucracy, no set curricula, and most of the Wisdom is imparted orally from teacher to tested-and-proven pupil. The inherent Truths are so universal, however, that you can recognize them across the globe and across the ages, once you know what you're looking at. Though usually kept secret and opened only to sincere seekers, the Wisdom Teachings are now being given to the world in general, in hopes of affecting positive changes in humankind.

mysticism - the emotional, feeling approach to life, initiation, character and spiritual growth; as opposed to the mental, rational, occult approach. Most religions have a mystic branch: Gnostic Christians, Sufi Muslims, Jewish Cabalists, etc.

mythology - the stories we tell ourselves to explain the world around us and within us. It's said that a "true myth" will resonate with truth on at least seven different levels such as: physiological, sociological, psychological, historical, philosophical, geological, cosmological, astrological, astronomical, chemical, evolutionarily, and now with the incredible revelations of subatomic physics and quantum mechanics.

occult - means hidden. It does not mean evil. The Wisdom Teachings used to be kept hidden because it is powerfully effective, and if done without proper training and motivation, can be dangerous to the self and others. To be on the Occult Path implies study, mental work, step-by-step logical progression as opposed to the more emotional Mystic Path.

Persia - the old name for the country called Iran since 1935. Persians are not Arabs/Semitic; they are Aryan and thus related to Indians and Caucasians/Europeans.

Sanskrit - the sacred language of old India. Some say its words were designed to have specific effects, so mantras and names are "magical" The same is also said of Latin, which is related to Sanskrit. The liturgy of the Catholic Mass was also supposedly designed to have certain affects via the sounds of the words.

SETI - Search for Extra Terrestrial Intelligence. An organization conducting scientific research on life in the universe with an emphasis on intelligent life.

Shadow - an individual's more animal instincts, that pre-conscious part of the self. Dr. Carl Jung saw it as the unexpressed parts of ourselves we often project onto others.

soul - conscious awareness, sentience.

spirit - the animating life force.

Sufi - a member of the mystical order of Islam, seeking direct union with Allah, the Merciful, the Compassionate.

Vedas - the holy-historical Sanskrit writings of the Hindus, Aryan peoples of northern India.

White Brotherhood – intelligent entities, sometimes human, who embrace and work for the unity of all Life.

Wisdom Teachings - see Ageless Wisdom and Mystery Schools.

Yahweh – Jehovah of the Old Testament.

ABOUT THE AUTHOR

Pamela Jaye Smith is a speaker, consultant, writer, award-winning producer-director, and the founder of MYTHWORKS. Credits and clients include Paramount, Disney, Microsoft, Universal, RAI-TV Rome, UCLA Ext. Writers Program, American Film Institute, USC Film School, Creative Screenwriting Expo, Pepperdine University, National  Film School of Denmark, Thot Fiction Marseilles France, Women in Film, GM, Boeing, the FBI, and the U.S. Army.

Pamela is a lifelong student of religion, science, and mythology. Growing up in a cattle ranching family in Texas, she was raised Catholic for ten years, then mainstream Protestant. She was exposed to Sufi mysticism in her early teens through her grandparents' extensive library and to other Asian philosophies through tales brought back by traveling relatives.

Though she started in premed and music, Pamela received a B.A. with a major in English, minor in Latin, and secondary studies in Radio-TV-Film at the University of Texas, Austin. She studied Buddhism with novelist Professor Raja Rao and Sri Krishna Menon, a colleague of Joseph Campbell. Continually searching for the science behind mystical experiences, she came upon the Ageless Wisdom — the Physics of Metaphysics and heart of all mystery schools. After seven years of formal study, Pamela became a certified Wisdom teacher.

As a filmmaker for 30-plus years in Hollywood, having worked at the major studios, large corporations, and wildly independent productions, she has experienced first-hand the evil excesses of power, money, and ego — without falling prey to them herself, of course.

Besides weathering tornadoes in Texas, earthquakes, riots and celebrity trials in LA, and minus 80° temperatures in the Arctic oil fields, world travels have often plunged Pamela into perilous situations where the Dark Side looms threateningly close, such as rappelling down cliffs and skirting the fringes of third world revolutions, with kidnappers and machete-wielding crazies lurking nearby. Then there were the ornate five-star hotels with temptations such as cold gin-and-tonics and fresh fist-sized prawns.

Participation in a U.S. Army think tank (the Advanced Warfighting Working Group out of Fort Knox), attending both Army and Air Force War Colleges National Security Forums, and pursuing military intelligence studies have exposed Pamela to the more formal approaches to conflict.

Various projects have found her dealing with corporate and government personnel, including the U.S. State Department and U.S. Embassies here and abroad, Chinese and other foreign Embassies, NASA/Jet Propulsion Laboratory, the Smithsonian Air and Space Museum, Pan American Airlines, McDonnell Douglas, provincial Governors, and tribal chieftains.

She is an avid reader, drives a '77 Bronco, and enjoys opera. A dilettante approach to sports has included surfing, skiing, snorkeling, flying, go-cart & auto racing, and driving an off-shore oil rig and an Army tank – both under close supervision.

Pamela is a member of Lodge New Isis, George Washington Union, a Masonic Obedience working in North America that accepts men and women on an equal basis. She was in the Millennial edition of

Who's Who in the World, and she is a card-carrying member of the California Emergency Response Team.

For story consultations, writing, speaking engagements, and lots more about myth and media, visit Pamela's MYTHWORKS website *www.mythworks.net*.

MORE MYTHIC TOOLS™
TO HELP YOU IMPROVE
YOUR CREATIVITY AND YOUR CRAFT

INNER DRIVES

How to Write and Create Characters
Using the Eight Classic Centers of Motivation
Michael Wiese Productions *www.mwp.com*

BEYOND THE HERO'S JOURNEY

Other Powerful Mythic Themes
MYTHWORKS *www.mythworks.net*

PITCHING TIPS FROM ANCIENT AUTHORS

MYTHWORKS *www.mythworks.net*

SEMINAR AND WORKSHOP CDs AND TAPES:
ALPHA BABES, ARCHEPATHS, BEYOND THE HERO'S
JOURNEY, CREATING OUR NEXT MYTHS, and many more
MYTHWORKS *www.mythworks.net*

STORY CONSULTATIONS, WRITING, COACHING
SPEAKER, TEACHER
www.mythworks.net

INNER DRIVES
HOW TO WRITE AND CREATE CHARACTERS USING THE EIGHT CLASSIC CENTERS OF MOTIVATION

PAMELA JAYE SMITH

Inspiring and practical, *Inner Drives* goes to the very source of character motivation and action. Exploring the fascinating world of archetypes, mythology, and the chakra system, writers will learn to apply timeless principles of successful storytelling through fascinating examples and valuable exercises.

From patterns of speech to styles of walking, writers can use Pamela Jaye Smith's guide to structure character arcs, devise backstories, up the conflict, pair up couples, and form ensembles — all with unique, believable characters.

Informative and entertaining, this book helps writers, directors, designers, development executives, and actors expand their artistry and influence on the audience to gain a creative advantage in a highly competitive industry.

"In *Inner Drives*, Pamela Jaye Smith has created a masterpiece that magically combines myth with motivation, the use of chakras in the craft of writing, and self-exploration as an integral part of storytelling. Whether you are writing your masterpiece, or just trying to better understand yourself and those you interact with, *Inner Drives* will give you the intimate intricate detail you need to grasp the universal realities of Planet Hollywood, and indeed of Planet Earth."
> — Lynn Santer, Author, *Sins of Life, Into the Fire, Evil by Design*;
> Filmmaker, *Lewis's Piano*

"Pamela Jaye Smith's *Inner Drives* is written for screenwriters, but will be welcomed by everyone from novelists to TV sitcom writers. It explores what makes a character tick, the choices one person may make compared to another, and the deep structure of character. Highly readable with plenty of story examples, this wonderful book will make new or experienced writers very happy."
> — Mollie Gregory, Author, *Women Who Run the Show - How A*
> *New Generation Stormed Hollywood, Making Films Your Business,*
> *Triplets, Birthstone, Privileged Lies*

PAMELA JAYE SMITH is a writer, mythologist, consultant, speaker, and award-winning producer/director with international clients and credits in features, TV, commercials, music videos, documentaries, and corporate films.

$26.95 · 264 PAGES · ORDER NUMBER 32RLS · ISBN: 9781932907032

Our books are all about helping you create memorable films that will move audiences for generations to come.

Since 1981, we've published over 100 books on all aspects of filmmaking which are used in more than 600 film schools around the world. Many of today's most productive filmmakers and writers got started with our books.

According to a recent Nielsen BookScan analysis, as a publisher we've had more best-selling books in our subject category than our closest competitor – and they are backed by a multi-billion dollar corporation! This is evidence that as an independent – filmmaker or publisher – you can create the projects you have always dreamed of and earn a livelihood.

To help you accomplish your goals, we've expanded our information to the web. Here you can receive a 25% discount on all our books, buy the newest releases before they hit the bookstores, and sign up for a newsletter which provides all kinds of new information, tips, seminars, and more. You'll also find a Virtual Film School loaded with articles and websites from our top authors, teacher's guides, video streamed content, free budget formats, and a ton of free valuable information.

We encourage you to visit www.mwp.com. Sign up and become part of a wider creative community.

Onward and upward,
Michael Wiese
Publisher, Filmmaker

If you'd like to receive a free MWP Newsletter,
click on www.mwp.com to register.

FILM & VIDEO BOOKS
TO RECEIVE A FREE MWP NEWSLETTER, CLICK ON WWW.MWP.COM TO REGISTER

SCREENWRITING | WRITING

And the Best Screenplay Goes to... | Dr. Linda Seger | $26.95

Archetypes for Writers | Jennifer Van Bergen | $22.95

Cinematic Storytelling | Jennifer Van Sijll | $24.95

Could It Be a Movie? | Christina Hamlett | $26.95

Creating Characters | Marisa D'Vari | $26.95

Crime Writer's Reference Guide, The | Martin Roth | $20.95

Deep Cinema | Mary Trainor-Brigham | $19.95

Elephant Bucks | Sheldon Bull | $24.95

Fast, Cheap & Written That Way | John Gaspard | $26.95

Hollywood Standard, The | Christopher Riley | $18.95

I Could've Written a Better Movie than That! | Derek Rydall | $26.95

Inner Drives | Pamela Jaye Smith | $26.95

Joe Leydon's Guide to Essential Movies You Must See | Joe Leydon | $24.95

Moral Premise, The | Stanley D. Williams, Ph.D. | $24.95

Myth and the Movies | Stuart Voytilla | $26.95

Power of the Dark Side, The | Pamela Jaye Smith | $22.95

Psychology for Screenwriters | William Indick, Ph.D. | $26.95

Rewrite | Paul Chitlik | $16.95

Romancing the A-List | Christopher Keane | $18.95

Save the Cat! | Blake Snyder | $19.95

Save the Cat! Goes to the Movies | Blake Snyder | $24.95

Screenwriting 101 | Neill D. Hicks | $16.95

Screenwriting for Teens | Christina Hamlett | $18.95

Script-Selling Game, The | Kathie Fong Yoneda | $16.95

Stealing Fire From the Gods, 2nd Edition | James Bonnet | $26.95

Way of Story, The | Catherine Ann Jones | $22.95

What Are You Laughing At? | Brad Schreiber | $19.95

Writer's Journey, – 3rd Edition, The | Christopher Vogler | $26.95

Writer's Partner, The | Martin Roth | $24.95

Writing the Action Adventure Film | Neill D. Hicks | $14.95

Writing the Comedy Film | Stuart Voytilla & Scott Petri | $14.95

Writing the Killer Treatment | Michael Halperin | $14.95

Writing the Second Act | Michael Halperin | $19.95

Writing the Thriller Film | Neill D. Hicks | $14.95

Writing the TV Drama Series – 2nd Edition | Pamela Douglas | $26.95

Your Screenplay Sucks! | William M. Akers | $19.95

FILMMAKING

Film School | Richard D. Pepperman | $24.95

Power of Film, The | Howard Suber | $27.95

PITCHING

Perfect Pitch – 2nd Edition, The | Ken Rotcop | $19.95

Selling Your Story in 60 Seconds | Michael Hauge | $12.95

SHORTS

Filmmaking for Teens | Troy Lanier & Clay Nichols | $18.95

Ultimate Filmmaker's Guide to Short Films, The | Kim Adelman | $16.95

BUDGET | PRODUCTION MGMT

Film & Video Budgets, 4th Updated Edition | Deke Simon & Michael Wiese | $26.95

Film Production Management 101 | Deborah S. Patz | $39.95

DIRECTING | VISUALIZATION

Animation Unleashed | Ellen Besen | $26.95

Citizen Kane Crash Course in Cinematography | David Worth | $19.95

Directing Actors | Judith Weston | $26.95

Directing Feature Films | Mark Travis | $26.95

Fast, Cheap & Under Control | John Gaspard | $26.95

Film Directing: Cinematic Motion, 2nd Edition | Steven D. Katz | $27.95

Film Directing: Shot by Shot | Steven D. Katz | $27.95

Film Director's Intuition, The | Judith Weston | $26.95

First Time Director | Gil Bettman | $27.95

From Word to Image | Marcie Begleiter | $26.95

I'll Be in My Trailer! | John Badham & Craig Modderno | $26.95

Master Shots | Christopher Kenworthy | $24.95

Setting Up Your Scenes | Richard D. Pepperman | $24.95

Setting Up Your Shots, 2nd Edition | Jeremy Vineyard | $22.95

Working Director, The | Charles Wilkinson | $22.95

DIGITAL | DOCUMENTARY | SPECIAL

Digital Filmmaking 101, 2nd Edition | Dale Newton & John Gaspard | $26.95

Digital Moviemaking 3.0 | Scott Billups | $24.95

Digital Video Secrets | Tony Levelle | $26.95

Greenscreen Made Easy | Jeremy Hanke & Michele Yamazaki | $19.95

Producing with Passion | Dorothy Fadiman & Tony Levelle | $22.95

Special Effects | Michael Slone | $31.95

EDITING

Cut by Cut | Gael Chandler | $35.95

Cut to the Chase | Bobbie O'Steen | $24.95

Eye is Quicker, The | Richard D. Pepperman | $27.95

Invisible Cut, The | Bobbie O'Steen | $28.95

SOUND | DVD | CAREER

Complete DVD Book, The | Chris Gore & Paul J. Salamoff | $26.95

Costume Design 101 | Richard La Motte | $19.95

Hitting Your Mark – 2nd Edition | Steve Carlson | $22.95

Sound Design | David Sonnenschein | $19.95

Sound Effects Bible, The | Ric Viers | $26.95

Storyboarding 101 | James Fraioli | $19.95

There's No Business Like Soul Business | Derek Rydall | $22.95

FINANCE | MARKETING | FUNDING

Art of Film Funding, The | Carole Lee Dean | $26.95

Complete Independent Movie Marketing Handbook, The | Mark Steven Bosko | $39.95

Independent Film and Videomakers Guide – 2nd Edition, The | Michael Wiese | $29.95

Independent Film Distribution | Phil Hall | $26.95

Shaking the Money Tree, 2nd Edition | Morrie Warshawski | $26.95

OUR FILMS

Hardware Wars: DVD | Written and Directed by Ernie Fosselius | $14.95

On the Edge of a Dream | Michael Wiese | $16.95

Sacred Sites of the Dalai Lamas– DVD, The | Documentary by Michael Wiese | $24.95

LaVergne, TN USA
20 September 2009
158283LV00003BA/2/P